T0279501

as mornings and mossgreen I.
Step to the window

THE GERMAN LIST

Friederike Mayröcker

as mornings and mossgreen I.
Step to the window

TRANSLATED BY ALEXANDER BOOTH

LONDON NEW YORK CALCUTTA

This publication was supported by a grant from the Austrian Federal Ministry for Education, Arts and Culture, and the Goethe-Institut India.

Seagull Books, 2023

Originally published in German as *da ich morgens und moosgrün. Ans Fenster trete* by Friederike Mayröcker

© Suhrkamp Verlag, Berlin, 2020
All rights reserved by and controlled through
Suhrkamp Verlag, Berlin

First published in English translation by Seagull Books, 2023
English translation © Alexander Booth, 2023

ISBN   978 1 8030 9 142 6

British Library Cataloguing-in-Publication Data
A catalogue record for this book is available from
the British Library

Typeset by Seagull Books, Calcutta, India
Printed and bound by WordsWorth India, New Delhi, India

as mornings and mossgreen I.
Step to the window

for Edith S.

on the swallowlandscape for Alfred K., the lit. lamb, I mean, the lit. white lamb in the blue (sky) execution of my conscience your voice a lit. white lamb in the blue (sky), you know, to sit beneath the canopy = cold already. Summer abated swallows migrated they'd extolled the sky above the hospital garden they were siblings my siblings, girding their breast a tender lead,

> in Alexander Wied's *Dream Journals* I come across an image from J. J. Grandville *An Animal in the Moon* which makes me tremble : I find myself confronted with a MOON FACE : an illness from which the poet Christine Busta also suffered = a wealth of leaves at the image's edge plunges into a sea of clouds (above the swallowlandscape your thumbnail moon seems to be sinking ......)

ever more frequently *c.* 3 or 4 in the morning have heard someone BREAKING IN. The bird isn't free : free the flower ballooning sun : purple hortensia : does it hear perhaps what I am saying what you are saying, is the lit. hand enough? in the corner the head of the palm, between the letter's pages your letter's the racing lines. The murmur of the spring there, back then, Bad Ischl by the current where we were overcome by tears, back then, the pianist in the restaurant's garden with the lit. dog on his lap, I mean, I had that delicate yap.

22.9.17

3

ach these semi-tones this lit. violetblue sky, after the opening-
of-the-eyes this morning he spotted such a rod = such an
antenna = such a glowing window = such a Mediterranean
mode of thought …… knock dish on a kitchen stool spotted,
so transcendent that from the distance you. That it's a conso-
lation that it's the whole of my happiness in the morning, that
a white plastic cup *with a handle* the whole of my happiness that
the world shatters into pieces, etc., I mean, in the throat *cherries*
cherryred love. I buy 2 dozen of them in the junk shop press
them to my heart, Chairos, the worms and I! Tuberose tea rose
(yellow), he shows me this their turn of the head to the right,
that is, the whole of my happiness : white plastic cup *with a han-
dle*, whispering palm leaf at the flat door : pleated woman's
dress in green, Mama's sleeves, crust of blood on her lit. mouth,
she was an aesthete, was knotting a kelim, my hearing threat-
ened to break down : at 3 in the morning I heard someone
breaking in, my vermilion dishevelled ear, no not deaf but *dusty
ear*, I've bought Edmond Jabès' *Book of Questions*, in the stair-
well ran into Gottfried Haider wearing HALO, lovely angel.
Blinded by his azure, namely,

> these days rather miserable, remembering chatting
> with friend Alexander W. along the banks of the
> Traun and walking,

hearing the Rolling Stones they were,

I flashed him a sign : come-hither in the super-
market he

was supposed to come and look ('come and see!') I had come
across a yng. potted palm and beckoned him with my finger
and he hurried over and we took it and it became our paletot
secret too,

how the lit. breeze blustered, petered out, wolfish
summer (barefoot over the path through the conifer-
ous woods),

Hurricane (Lilian) Harvey : 9.9.17, and I'm telling you in 4
months the sapling'll be back and *needling*,

ring in the ear or wildflower (howling),

23.9.17

Bertolt Brecht wrote a most beautiful most German poem about a white cloud and a seventh child over which I often wept. It had to do with a white cloud breaking apart while lying with a woman in a meadow, on the day a man stepped foot on the moon I was lying in a meadow with a man whose chest was encircled by a delicate lead, from whose mouth a thin blade of grass,

in a fevermonth, 28.9.17

in the morning FOOL'S GOLD in my fists. Dear Bastian my health frail ach!, from literacy to painting you must know that I have long aspired to connect 'avant-gardism' to 'classicism' ...... I owe you a lot : enbushed by a thirst for knowledge and intuition I can't stop portraying the world of love,

> the lit. walnut tree in Schiller Park, you know, how long now aflower and fragrant. Lilac jasmine ach their blooming so short = youth, duck feathers' lovely colours, back then, I scream, you said 'back when I was a boy' ...... contemplative this kelim = mother's handiwork on the wall in the room where I dream, etc. Gerhard Rühm's *teleklavier*

these 2 weeks were disastrous, I mean, I'm speechless. I watched all the nuns watering the dried-out flowerbeds, in the evening,

> dear Isel, paint me a FANTASIA of Madrid that the heart in its chamber, a lot of windows with a view onto a couple of Alps, namely, a moribund summer, I collapsed 3 X today, like overpainted red peonies, you know,

> *tear the silk of one last morning.*

1.10.17

ach as detached from this speech that one acquiesced to love. Really, all the way through your flesh your beautiful soul appears to me, can I snatch it? it the secretive clever that lovely the rain falls 'when the eyes practice', tear the silk of one last morning,

for a doctor by the name of B.

1.10.17

then we fell around each other's necks, namely. A small pastel of a Matisse, back then, a formation of winter birds, as one next to the other we bent out the window, a medium! what! lightblue cloudeye, you know, halved : in gusts picked flowers from the window, my snowshoes : broken shoes, ach an art-of-buds Giotto-trees a drainage-of-blooms, latest buzzword 'exciting', you turn your head like a bird, namely, he turned his head like a bird, *namely, to the right* so that I asked him 'like a bird?' he was, namely, a bird, it was 11 o'clock and the night sky, as one next to the other at the window, touching each other, and the night sky, namely, sank, Fauré's *Requiem* to love, as if A CAULIFLOWER wanted a SAPLING, in the vase with a glowing glance, etc., on a step I think a salamander and as it sparkled,

> this lightblue heaven's eye, from winds, dishevelled, more-or-less, I'm attached to this *conceptualism* of Kurt Ryslavy's = 2 upside-down stools in a room,

had epi-attacks had gone out of myself, ach, pre-historic animals (in the Museum of Cadiz) : a red rooster with ochre-coloured tailfeathers, a snail shell, a quadruped,

> LIT. SPIRIT, that eternally there, a lock, a lock of your hair,

> 5.10.17

Canzone in praise of love based on a photograph from Arnulf Rainer's atelier,

in a photograph; in a photograph from Arnulf Rainer's atelier a cut-off rocking chair or white bag on black canvas or white dove on black canvas climbing white dove or a sketch with its face to the wall of Arnulf Rainer's atelier, namely, with its face to the wall : pastel-coloured painting, would have liked to be; a painter, *namely*, *maison*. Namely, how the moon sank into the river in a corner of the dream of Arnulf Rainer's atelier, that is, a depiction of his face, whereas I whispered embellishment to a poem 'it rained into my heart,' etc.,

ach I laid my head into the torn books on
the floor,
the birds clutch at elderberries and I found a half-open nut where a branch was beginning to sprout, canzone in praise of love based on a photograph from Arnulf Rainer's atelier,

(let's be off),

11.10.17

10

tsau! I say, tsau! my snorting, garden your white skin against my swiss-chard-heart, once whirling. I'm in hospital Room 401 shimmering pigeon plumage in the hospital garden see oil and vinegar and blood, of a bitten-into plum ...... 37° gown (temperature), blindly a summer shower. My fly-like (ach) torso, I'm lonely my comrade an old dog, me death's debutante, stony my final way to where Mother and Father and friend etc., on these Rechnitz mountains, still sinful the world and vain, let us remain undaunted, you say, hair and teeth fallen out *earlier we were flowers*, Ovid perhaps, Naso. Well now, rabbit fur about the neck, a lit. brook in my room (more or less) meadow (!), Father floated a lit., into the open air, Arnulf Rainer's *Rükkenkratʒen* : oil on cardboard 73 X 102 cm = lit. garden aflame in red, etc.,

> back then, Father, chatting on Kärtnerstrasze, when someone poked his shoulder blade, when Father turned around, 3 weeks before his *going*, no one was there ...... furry leaves, I mean, *opaque white* of blind edelweiss,

> spring-footed the sun : scurried, the sun, past : behind curtains past, likewise mola mola,

12.10.17

Horde of texts or tableaux, to G.R., more or less, constructivist
poet in Cologne on the Rhine, etc.,

in that photo he was sitting PLAYING PIANO so far away
from the instrument that upon one's tongue the word longing.

Longing for wings intoxication of a great bird, do you
know what a rocker blotter (is), Ovid or Naso thicket of an
eyelash,

I mean, tearing open one's breast like a falcon. Feeds. Its young.
A lit. Matisse hung in the salon where the concert piano stood,
have we betrayed the figurative?,

'I've got no idea what that's supposed to mean' I saw
the Rhine inside me, mantilla, namely, ruffles from
Vienna.

17.10.17

I'd lost it in my flat they were lost I couldn't find them again
they were a piece of me but the sentences had got lost, I let my
eye rest on the shapes of my room once again find the strangest
objects, those I'd been looking for too, the gentian ach how it
fevers against my words, one says evening red but morning
redness, etc., as if at every 3. line I wanted to swing around the
corner, it spooned so silvery blue in the early morning, that is,
in the window. A lit. of this puffed-up tufted-up sitting together
with friends so brushed-up, like a hairdo ...... these tiny hairs
on the tile floor (bathroom) the mixed portraits already fra-
grant, I gave him a lectern for Easter!, where he was supposed
to write like a Goethe, *ach beaked snow, etc.,*

> the ground's already cooling down, white
> cloud-wigs oh cloud-beloved how your dis-
> appearance lasts, the forest of this

beloved deep shrouded sealed passed away, my hand my mouth
are looking for you ...... the memory delightful, the moss with
naked feet, the moss, *enraptured* this book I.

> Where can I find roe deer are you roe? some
> poem or other lying on the floor : these words
> always slipping away from me, so, lit. tongue,
> I'm worried about you, as if the vanished
> word : the vanished words turned up again :
> but it was only *a wisp or wound,*

one time the friend = Leo Navratil was among the mourners
another time he himself was buried. One had a steep set of
stairs, up. to climb,

> all she brought back from Japan was one tiny red
> cushion, stuck to a clothes peg painted with blossoms,
> *die verregneten kirschen* (Helmut Federle 2009)

this infanta of a landscape. How we played footsie, back then!,

4.11.17

corner étude, ach spotted 2 yng. trees, one bent with a pair of lips or *Soffa* in its midst (yew in the window!), on to the feast-for-the-eyes = in hospital the eye doctor was named Dr Freude —I said goodbye with the words 'Freude schöner Götter-funken' which she took SOMEWHAT poorly, etc., in response to the question how she could carry such a heavy heart the princess,

> a gingko leaf sinks to the ground and Goethe, I mean, Goethe beside it, one of the nurses had a metre-long, braid. Ach did she remain overhead?

this Küfferle, with gloomy eye, etc.,

5.11.17

these grains of rice across the parquet, Chenal or chapeau or cheval, I mean, she was standing under the blue strapped. At the door to her shop, and was looking into the blue strapped. Perhaps a shovel of air, etc., she had dreamt of all the heavenly, I mean, idylls she was my grandmother I take after her,

> there was indeed something there, a tear = in
> a letter a lit. horse in a letter a lit. horse in a
> letter, etc., but the lit. horse tore open your
> cheek so that your flesh (dearest!), I saw how

your flesh : lit. shreds of flesh ...... I'm drawing you a tear beneath your eye my tongue an autumn crocus upon your lid yes I am perhaps a muffin and consent to be being eaten (by your eye),

> your eye a grey cloud grey pearl grey diamond : able
> to speak in soft languages, namely, a tear sinks *into a*
> *bundle of grass*, etc.,

you've knotted a kelim you've knotted a tiger that had, the face of a human,

> there all aflame : Arnulf Rainer's *Rückenkratzen*
> red claws.

CROISETTE,

once said, Durs Grünbein, he wanted to do a reading with me on the moon, etc., *whereas I*, a lit. dishevelled,

> *in every line whereas, a flower*, nights uncomfortable.

7.11.17

the climbing, back then, you know, up the slope, the stunted lit. tree which no more fruit. Dear Siegfried the group photo with Gabriele Rothemann makes me really happy, her *Waterfall* rips open memories of childhood holidays! you look really elegant with your wavy hair! (so much going on in Meran), when Fabi in Vienna? as a yng. girl did I wear big black bows in my hair? so that I (more or less) looked like a moth ...... my sneakers how I love you, to feel my experiences or (to) *conjure*, the completely extinguished brimstone butterfly, my survival lottery, WINTER'S IMP already closer, *Evening by the River* that upon a lit. bench while the full moon, behind the mountains, I mean, sank I am writing by moonlight *enraptured* (in the moonlight) = noblesse of paper, etc., I can't get the roller blinds in my bedroom down so that the morning sun, my face, scratches,

are you a wind conductor this morning?

11.11.17

Ingrid Wald : screen pastel-sky before I go to sleep at night I dream of water and spray and rockets of rain, of the blurring of a poem, etc., ach, I say, a few grasshoppers between the pages of your letter. She was, when painting, within a SEPA-RATION = in heaven, in the evening I sit in black-yellow wallpaper (Tapete), erasing : I nodded off *as in the doorway you* and you saw that I'd nodded off, from the distance I saw a cactus in your picture, from a distance felt the sting of a cactus in your picture, *Roter Berg* : 1962–78 oil on canvas 100 X 75 cm, composition with white fleck, *I mean, the snowy air*, the blue the summer scurried past, flowerbed in red (dumbfounded futurum),

> this dove pattering (namely) : nude descend-ing a staircase, I mean, Duchamp, back then. In the vanished years did we ever pick autumn crocus on the Cobenzl when summer : when summer began to tilt, dimly, autumn's edge, etc.,

bunches blooms purple blooms, bunches tears, delicate bunches of roe deer, *icons*,

22.11.17

Poussin's 'empire of flora', I mean, smarthistory,

whenever the name PURKERSDORF falls I think of
stag beetles blown ginko leaf *railway* above all railway,
I mean, the lit. scattered houses and beloved gardens
across the hills,
the girl's name FLORA like a lit. fork ψ I draw Flora
= lit. fork like lit. fork = ψ lit. silver fork. In
all the pubs he'd always stick the lit. silver fork
into : ψ ψ ψ ψ then we'd laugh a lit., perhaps lace-
work, you know, I mean, *praying underground*, you
know, praying underground, ach, wren nature's pleat,
half-asleep Andreas O. blew me lit. kisses, and at
breakfast the tears rolled down, I mean, the tears they
rolled down ...... into a white plastic cup with a
handle, I love it so! press it to my heart, my pleated
one, childhood, etc.

we were talking about weeping, no, says Erika T., she cannot
cry any more, she cried a lot when she was young, *but now she
is made of stone*, if she used to cry a lot if in the past she used to
be able to cry now she is frozen : no tears, so Erika T., but I see
a tear before me : a crying fish or Fuji. Well yeah, maybe the
shedding of tears is a shedding of blood, a weeping carnation
or palm's pleat, as beautiful as a frond a tear shed, as beautiful
as cypress,

object representation we hunt against the horrible
winter sun. Back then, at the cardiologist, I'd STUFF

his sweaty underclothes into my handbag, in a corner
of the waiting room a plastic potted palm,

then, having wandered long and *transparent*

23.11.17

'from out of my mouth I discharged the
shadowy Alpenvalley'

ach the lit. letter to * = dear reader dear child's head, the
2. time, namely, on the 2. morning I awoke with the word

PENKALA

which conjures a smile, I mean, I feel a smile that says 'good
morning, just who or what's Penkala?' but a few tears as well it
seems to me that I can remember the hour of my birth the
glimpse of my beautiful yng. mother as well as the midwife's cry
'dearestangel lit.childofgod' : a winter afternoon in '24 ......
how can it be that I remember my father saying I was an ugly
baby because I was yellow. Perhaps I *feigned all the colours*
Chinese colours gasped for breath, maybe homebirth the most
comprehensive drapery, etc.,

> 6 years later Gerhard Rühm, born he said to me no
> that idea had not occurred to him that the word 'long-
> ing' flowed onto my tongue whereas in his perfor-
> mance : in his performance he SHOWED that ¼ m
> away from his steinway he could play his instrument,
> everything (everywhere) so damp the grass sprouted
> through the white tablecloth, you know, for more than
> 2 hours I've been TRYING to form this phrase, I
> mean, until I (start to) scream,

'*Inkwell*' scream inkwell,
hobbling night.

24.11.17

whenever I read the word BIEL I think of the *Vision of the Hedge*! where Heinz Schafroth used to sit in his study = wildrose shrub, I mean, *hide*, whenever I called Ruth Schafroth would answer from her kitchen ...... hedge estate in late bloom, etc., such blue rags upon the horizon, ach, my self-neglect, copying out old books I once wrote, early this morning opening my eyes was it an illumination that I was sitting in Heinz Schafroth's living room like years before and looking out onto Lake Biel (namely, so pale!), which blinked and flashed into my eyes and that I went silent,

> but for weeks in tears ...... well yeah, I'd run into Gottfried H. in the stairwell, I mean, I'd almost literally run into him, I hardly recognized him, wearing a crosshatched wool cap,

back then winter '88, they hoisted him over the cornices, out in front of the Sofiensaal, some kind of MEDUSAS, on the pavements, the waterfalls in Slunj, etc., once he asked me 'are you still crying?',

29.11.17

(this accurate, no, abstract poetry, etc.),

'the kitchen's fluttering'he said / he said 'wheezing like gera-
niums in a lit. window garden,' once he said 'your charming
kitchen', I am now already so praised in my buses the lit. pink
cloud of my buses, etc., the lit. lush cloud of my buses.

PEEPED into the vis-à-vis window, saw person
female person with mopping industry, mob or mopping with a
wet broom (jingled), this scraping in the early morning
Ingeborg in the first place Ingeborg, in the early morning
winterlike shovelling shovelling snow as if a violet snow =
bouquet of violets sparkling in winter, the word violet, always
on the pavements, namely, the wild tears, *some kind of Medusas*,
and I was shaken

once discreet by this spangled winter, yellow hair source, still
12 months to live, such a spangled winter : trickling down the
window,

in a shopping net. Rachel Salamander, in a
shopping net loud white flowers (of winter's blooms, of winter's
flakes, of winter's tears), for a long time now already = for a
long time now the birds unhappiness the birds shocks ......
back then, he'd leaf through the steadfast bookshelves in his
den! *I smiled at him*, already flashing, partout, the illumination
ach loud plastic baskets with Jacques Derrida, e.g.,

reading = the white lilac = Ezra Pound,
again, I love the word again ach how I love

this word or the word elsewhere how I love
the word elsewhere

which always a bit sweaty, so SCHWITTERS, I mean, from
out of his mighty skull the spines of *Schwitters* and *Finnegans
Wake* towered, like the midges, you know, like lit. branches of
narration,

*deaf and stiff and left knee and going in the
wash.*

1.12.17

'OP-addiction, it flakes it flakes, the devil, should go and fetch winter, this poet's : Francis Ponge, lit. line teeth, I don't often know which word it is and which words, from whence the word from whence the word from whence the words *ach*, *as if grabbed from out of the air*, something, and you said 'what a spangled winter!' it was as if a. cauliflower sapling in a vase, whispering, passionate bust BUSTA (bag) of a bouquet, pleated women's dress in green : beloved head of palm, I *invented* these lines at 4 o'clock in the morning, of a mild win-ter's coloratura, you know, I mean, 'nuages gris' for solo piano by Franz Liszt, broken, snowdrop, perhaps, ach a breeze *of*. I write long lists *of*, those words that get and got LOST! ......

> ach you gave me a swiss pine, a swiss pine heart a
> swiss pine spirit, *Ponge*, *writing about a glass of water*,
> the white shards snowdrops in withered grass,

indeed a smudged red mouth painted on the wall in the stairwell who *smothered* you with kisses who kissed your smudged red mouth, lit. spirit! racing through the woods in a rage

> (he's from Korneuburg, you know, where the corn-
> flowers,
> > *summers*)
> > > *along a stretch of water*,

5.12.17

that lit. spring, by the wine stand, back then, in Bad Ischl ......
if I ever something green, back then in the thin enclosed weed
garden where the spring ach the lit. spring, as if crushed the grass
a broken, lit. drop of snow or lily of the valley, how I
ENMESHED it with the threads of a love ach this lit. spring
how it tumbled and sprayed, at that lit. corner where a salaman-
der, perhaps, perhaps it was a different time of year, perhaps it
was an azure winter, he was already ill could barely toddle his
way down the stairs, could barely toddle his way down,

> *painted*! landscape format, these winter
> blooms how I shivered, how I cursed, the
> memory to write about a swarm of gnats I
> stood there still the leafless halls I stood there
> still a grove of thistles, he shimmered he
> slumbered : a salamander upon the path
> through the meadow,

a bitter field, you know,

> *a miserere-mom in the woods*!

reading = the white lilac, so Ezra Pound, back then in winter
'98, they hoisted him over the cornices : bellowing cornices
out in front of the Sophiensaal, we shed the pale, tears : the pale
rose of the field rosy medusas, ach how the long bygone : flown
snow, at 8 o'clock in the morning the tiger Norway ready to
spring, my medicine abuse, the heart's plume (feathering), she

wanted to have my poem framed as if it were a violet (bouquet) namely, in love. I mean, how the lines of my poem come loose from the branches of a tree, or bush ......

that there, the friends,

                                     6.12.17, the wet teats
                                     of shuttered
                                     ice-cream shops,

and thought JELLY : *the jelly of a moon*, back then, by that
budding-walk budding-crucifixion (= Nice), a branch brushed
my shoulder,

> I dreamt of walking barefoot over stones but
> they were something braids : gravel, of heel
> spur,

it happened (what a word!) that early evening when the yellow
moon raised itself I thought of the yellow banana-mouth or
moon, namely, the enraptured MOONSHINE that moved me,
suspected, I, that the dearest one ('embroidered hobby!') kissed
the left shoulder, so I turned around to see : which pair of lips,
had kissed me, touched : my eucharist, etc.,

> I dreamt of the painter Andreas Grunert that
> he'd painted *half a dog, blurry season,*

back then in Rome how time stranded in the bushes where the
tears = lemons. Unwedded ach the mussels ach kisses by the
sea, that a lit. branch brushed my shoulder, moved me (neck
or netherworld),

> I dreamt of the voice of the angels in the oaks
> so Adolf Wölfi in his Alpen world. *Dreamt
> I'd kicked the bucket,* and seen the cockatoo
> swing down,

laid awake for a long time last night formerly tongue-bouquet,

7.12.17

that I'd like to swallow the lit. plastic spoon, as well as knife with the bitten-off tip, *I mean*, *reverie*, see myself stumbling across snow-covered parkways (long-ago days), ach heralds of tears how we adore them, I'd like to become an ornithologist, I've got a polar *bird-nature*, you know, because Gottfried-going = namely, with my invalid's stick = walking stick is hard for me, I'd rather fly, ach milked Christmas, I'd like an eagle's eye in order to FEATHER : CATCH hidden treasure : *lines and roe deer,*

> there where the *branches* fork, the robin, I mean, the robin beaking ...... he, the American Germanist, didn't say 'standing ovations' but rather 'stehende Ovationen', I always liked Friedrich Schiller's way with the word fashion, I want to cry myself out just once all the way out, polar scuttling, I write prose with a lyrical *touch*, etc.

on the ceiling the wooden dove : circling, namely, floating from the top of its home all the way down, I mean, this particular white of whitest lilies with one Picasso of the most delicate green! Most delicate fan! the blind patient *recognized me by my gait.*

> Everywhere threads, of painting, to feel or conjure up my experiences, I mean, *to conjure* : I can taste this completion of language,

How odd how years ago I had a vision. Years ago my shoulder was brushed by a hedge it happened at the end of a summer,

years later a different hedge behind a different fence brushed
by other shoulder, in a garden of white blooms, and so I had to
wonder whether it was a passer-by who brushed me,

> 9.12.17, inspired :
> flying hare with
> crop,
> etc.,

'we'll fry in hell,' that's according to Seigried Höllrigl, kissed
this white decade, with your wavy hair, etc., I mean, kissed, a
moment of madness 3 blind edelweiss in the lit. glass with a
handle, this fledgling around the right eye (something like
chicory), it was an unconscious *boxing* against the right eye,
BROKEN snowdrop in this shoreless garden in Ischl, and there
was this bag with the swans, ach this tiny dream, your arms full
of flowers, etc.

> and whenever all the car alarms outside
> began to race I had to wonder whether you
> were safe, whereas down from the trees the
> stanzas tumbled, the wonderful stanzas drip-
> ping down from the trees or bushes, dumb-
> founded I was as if dumbfounded, the quartet
> : the blackbirds, namely, in the quartet,

at this point the word I use the most is 'no' I scream no! nasty
no. Up to saying no, Mr Beckett, these ranges! this lit. spring!
first cream! first snow! One book trails the next, then I was like
a partridge, *and had to stand in the corner*! I'm repeating myself,
early mass by Arnulf Rainer

> *I'm the devil's* it's snowing or raining, the
> Serbian nurse with her metre-long braid, one
> morning we ran into each other each with a
> smile, namely, the photo of a suspension
> bridge on the wall of the hospital lobby, after

a novel by Thornton Wilder (*The Bridge of San Luis Rey*),

darling fur mangy fur old fur, fidgeting in the garden or fidgeting in the malva garden; Erwin Bohatsch, *untitled*, 2000, tempera on paper 40 X 35 cm : cube clock with a curl, lit. left leg retracted, half past ten on the dial,

non-word of the year : *utter nonsense*!

I am androgynous how it rages inside my head! or deserts! My head a desert, in that very corner of my head it rages : it deserts, ach, wilderness of LANTERNS, I can see it before me in the '50s with Gerhard Rühm : motto motif or Monet. Young chimpanzees in a cage ...... the abstract leg of a young chimpanzee in a cage, *you're so sharp today* (scourging belly and Bauch etc.).

16.12.17, the hurricane
roaring so that it
knocked me down, at
midnight with
a tied-up sky,

'whereas writing just means sitting there and doing it : flight of
a winter bird (in the window), my notes slide off the chair, makes
a liquid-like sound, the word 'syringe' how beautiful it is how
much I love it (since forever!), tap the various groups, do good
work : invite your friends (?), delicate fan, how = we nested the
purple malva, in the spinach perhaps, a green half-moon

> my blurry face, the lit. green fur on the slopes
> of the Vienna Woods (Rubens' *The Lit. Fur*)
> DRUNK with being alone! what bloody col-
> oratura flood me! what unspeakables = hell-
> throats her head turned against mine, I say,
> Durs Grünbein's Inverness cape, 'I'd like to
> see you,' Durs Grünbein says, 'I'm invisible,'
> I say, gloomy lit. garden lit. alley by the river,

'dear Sarah thank you for the *lit. tablecloth* (testament) with
Elise and yew needles how fragrant! ach scribbling because
while writing the letter *doʒed off*, so that a sketch appeared =
yng. man with helmet and lit. bird, yesterday on the kitchen table
: yesterday on the kitchen table, 'pour Elise', almost choked
while eating cherries, as a passenger there the threatening sky
sank down (or sank). From somewhere or other an echo : I
caught an echo ...... when I saw Marcel Beyer speaking with
a crow in a photograph in conversation with a crow, I mean,
eye to eye I thought I could understand the conversation, the
bird's beak approaching the poet's eye that I FLINCHED in

fellow feeling, later I learnt : I learnt that the crow was stuffed, etc., whereas its natural siblings on the roof of a car.

Winter had come, or Elysium, on my two thumbs : the black of the ink ribbon, I mean,

I wish I could croak. Deep black.

23.12.17

full-moon with this ferret, Erwin Bohatsch, *untitled* : dial with flag and hoisted right foot, lit. foot (more or less) like that of a chest of drawers, *wasteland* : she possessed the head of a Gertrude Stein, aloe, namely, (night) privet, you lay the fir branch across my sheet as if your hand wanted to touch my mouth, namely, the weeping one, etc., ach February's fanfare, I mean, *totally Russian*, with this lit. wolf's fur = lonely wolf = Hans Hollein (†), I saw him with a *troop of his sons* on Stephansplatz, back then, crossing Stephansplatz, mightily. Calling me calling me by my baptismal name, with my wolf's collar, we met each other whereas on the steps to the cardiologist, well yeah, or the crescent moon,

> these great-aunts dressed in their rubber raincoats, a tad CAUSAL, where could I plant myself, in my new year of life, heart-servitude.

Hazy, you say, hazy bush tears, hazy bush violet blooms, roe deer, you say, the roe deer, went down the steps (Marcel Duchamp) ...... the colour of autumn crocus

> *Non-word of the year* : *utter nonsense*,

> 24.12.17, in that photo. he was sitting (playing piano) so far away from the instrument that one LONGING.

cryptic encounter, etc.

although not long ago a bit withdrawn (wasteland perhaps) I was pleased by your head of Gertrude Stein, I mean, the Christmas tree seller had 2 red lanterns, lit between the compositions (of the buildings), within

a famous air, etc.

24.12.17

While we were sitting together in the cafe you said 'I mean, not RAIN, I mean, DEW, for *the listening*' you say, a line for *the listening*, I am androgynous, how it *rages* in my head my head a waste, we always only saw each other when you a new ink ribbon into the machine, etc., Braque's frizzy hair, I mean, how the lines of a poem came loose from the branches of a tree or bush, rushing (!) wormed garden (from snakes!), when I told the doctor that I have to cry when I write he said, 'well yeah, tears in the morning : *world-soul* in the a.m. well yeah the lit. night boots, that by the end of August with raised arms, highly praised arms I was, how great green raindrops in the bushes ......' ach! Fresco in blue : your beautiful blue eyes,

> I whispered to you on the phone I whispered
> the word 'pointing' whereas down from the
> trees the stanzas tumble, down from the trees
> (more or less) the plovers, tumble, how
> *dumbfounded* I was, or bush, full of longing
> they dedicated a lilac bush on the lawn to me,

Lit. foot of a chest of drawers, namely. In D. I saw a lark which *gradually*, up and down, *fluttered*, you know.

(step into a sweatshop = Schweiszgeschäft)

6.1.18

Maybe he painted with a spoon like Goya snow and shadows in
the garden I'm going to feed the ravens now, ach, how smart
your atelier, your lit. horse with lng. hair, that is, with its wafer-
like, oleander cut ...... dear Man Ray you are my imaginary
friend my alter ego, ingenious your blue baguette! You're my
ready-made! Stepping into the therapy room of the psycho-
therapist E.S. the poster *noire et blanche* (1926) beamed at me,
I'd spent a few days with your biography so that I was dreaming
of you, I mean, as I stepped into the therapy room of the
psychotherapist E.S. the arms of a potted palm reached out its
arms. Just imagine dear Man Ray today the 25th of January
I found a letter you wrote to me 18 years ago (ach, you are
wearing an open speech-mantilla!), etc., Roger Shattuck wrote
about you : 'the silent artist and juggler had, so to speak, 3 inter-
changeable garments in his wardrobe : those of mystery, of
humour and of eroticism, sometimes he wore all 3 at the same
time' ...... You ask me how I am doing I say 'my inner life is
as before it's just that my corporeal life has become laborious' :
how now I wonder. Ach you are in fact a contemporary I can
take your hand as we patrol the palm garden of Sils Maria, such
an allegro of painting and photography, 'ganz easy' you said,
'ach the green flushes of nature', your longing-filled words on
the phone, you said photography was no art at all, in fact you
invented the poetic cinema, the film of chance, the film of illogic.
Kiki's artificial tears, Kiki's lips floating above the landscape,

you planted artificial tears on Kiki's face, you made *L'Étoile de mer*, *whisk MAN*,

honourable listeners do not attempt to disclose this text's secret

THE EXHIBITION IS OPEN

25.1.18

Sarah gave me a lit. tablecloth with a dedication as a gift, I dreamt that I caught a glimpse of a really sm. grave probably a child's grave on a street off the rural road in D. decorated with red flowers the burial mound with bright red flowers though normally a child's grave's in white. Or stud, etc., I was afraid of dying destitute, namely, I was afraid of becoming bedridden, namely, a fear of god, like dark ears of grain my eyebrow above my left eye, the latest buzzword 'nature-writing', M.S. wore a stormy curl which gave him a youthful appearance despite his age ...... lit. calendar '18 with a lit. white bookmark, curtains of snow, etc., I wake up with the words 'nouveau-riche village' and 'nouveau-riche villages',

please leave some of your clothes and linens with me I won't feel so abandoned and hounded by the night so damn long and anxiety-full, *I wouldn't be so destroyed* if only you left me a few of your bones / a few lit. clothes / a bit of hose a cap before flying off which I could cuddle my whole life long, etc., *I wouldn't be so destroyed* if only we could once again, in early spring, on the lit. wooden bench in front of our building, and raise our arms to the sky : such promises whereas coming home on the doormat a torn-open envelope *in whose throat.*

9/10 February 2018 : an asteroid flying just past the earth,

9.2.18

the beating heart of the text, of the animal, that is, 'I know the meadow where the primroses bloom,' so Anneke Brassinga, I mean, stuffing and stomping through the Emmental, etc., I wouldn't be so destroyed if the primroses were abloom on an early spring meadow, perhaps it was a drawing by Hieronymus Bosch *Tree Man* (1510–1515), I saw it at twilight : grass-green display window : ach wild eye-vegetables swirling churling in a display window : in the display window of the tailor Aslan Gültekin, I saw it at twilight, who told me that at twilight at daybreak (so) secretive (so) Matisse how the wallpaper overflows = vomits onto the table with flowers and apple, I mean, who told me that the garden was abloom broken snowdrop, let us go fleet-footed like candles = Afamia Al-Dayaa, that one is there such a doppelgänger such a clone,

> this torrent : these torrents of tears, O, end-
> less hour, was it a drawing by Hieronymous
> Bosch *Tree Man* 1510–1515 (more-or-less)
> early in the morning, I mean, Neckarhalde
> road in a white gown back then he was, he
> told me, roving about the realms of Hölderlin
> all night long to find a YNG : GIRL,

I wouldn't be so destroyed if I didn't always *doze off while writing a letter* resulting in a sketch e.g. *Yng. Mentor with Cap and Toil* well yeah, riddle of life, I mean, this light-green secret of musk moss and budding branches ach this natura of early spring in the tailor's display window. In another display window, a potted-plant box against the glass, namely, wanted to get free,

it landed my tear a single tear on my ring finger, etc., he said,
'you're a Hieronyma or owl upon a bare bush whereas grab-
bing a saying a sparrow with skittish feet from out of the air,
indeed delicate stork feet : on one foot, *skilful, etc.*' I thought
about it : a flaming moth, 'bigoted table', upon a yng. shimmer-
ing birch two lit. birds : thrushes, walking about the woods
bunched bent over ...... ever since I was 12 when playing
dodgeball,

11.2.18

ruffle of blooms. I write to my doctor, 'you expeller of souls! of evil spirits! if you were to feel all of your patients' anxieties inner turmoil *in the near future* you yourself would be. Bunched and bent over a bundle of lamentations, etc.,'

am I really so miserable now (illumined by moonlight : Heinrich Heine),

16.2.18

or a minnesinger. Or honeysuckle. Actually rather in love we sat out on the steps of the Burgtheater I pulled out a lit. notebook drew a pair of wings scribbling underneath 'should we go to Sweden? are the bells tolling?' another time in the dining hall of the Archduke Johann really warm, burnt, our nerves, I write to my doctor, 'you expeller of souls! of evil spirits! if you were to feel all of your patients' anxieties inner turmoil *in the near future* you yourself would be. Bunched and bent over a bundle of lamentations, etc.,' am I really so miserable now (illumined by moonlight : Heinrich Heine), I wouldn't be so destroyed if my curses landed upon Man Ray's painted flat iron with nails : 1921 / 1958, namely, *The Gift* or *Cadeau*, 15.3 X 9 X 11.4 cm, as you prefer,

> I wouldn't be so destroyed had my mother
> brought me into the world as an octopus, ach,
> may the ink of my blood flow into my poem,
> etc., as if I would wheel around the corner of
> my poem or a flower *block* my way so that
> into the *unimaginable* I, you know

you're heath-dog violet half-moon veiled weeping moon (above the trees) back then when we, night on the balcony of the Golden Ship Hotel and kissed ...... what kind of leaves. I wouldn't be so destroyed were the words / sentences / pansies / appearing as if in a dream disappeared again after a few moments, I mean, into which deep wells have they SUNK?

RUFFLE OF BLOOMS

A half-moon a veiled moon above the trees, I *pinched* my tongue so that screaming, I mean, stamping the ground with my foot, my texts come about through *reproductive eyes!* this text is an abstraction, you say, multiple times while writing the perspective changed, I mean, a pout, I sketched a dainty index finger, to point out a word, with a red fingernail, sometimes as if my friends caught me before I fell, ach. 'in my *soul*', I never imagined that I could in such a way. Namely, that symbol (I'd find) in his *blossoming* purse would (want to) circle around me,

in whose throat.

as if you were drawing my left eyebrow with a lit. dark branch, there in front of the window the curtains of snow, but I've been darkened with a dark soul! Lit. calendar '18 with a lit. white bookmark, the old spitting oven, the awkward swallow on the ceiling, circling, well yeah, I'd FALLEN IN LOVE with the silver penguin (on the backside of promo-ticket)! just like I'd FALLEN IN LOVE with the *fraying* blue calyxes of a corncockle ......

> Fernando Pessoa writes that a change of place is what you need *to feel*, no, I call out, on the contrary you've got to be rooted to the place where (more or less) a tintinnabulation of the footfalls of the dead,

the epiphany of a claw, namely,

...... an observation with *Jens Stupin* : if a name's slipped your memory or when you can only recall a first name = baptismal name it may happen that when the baptismal name is mentioned the *whole* name too appears. Which would not have appeared if someone had not uttered the baptismal name : experience of or with BH on a Sunday in Lent 17 February 2018 (wrapped in a fog-euphoria, etc.),

17.2.18

support of the ears, or blessed words, or variation on sorrow etc.

when I think of Cologne I think of Lorelei, with her
golden hair : sweet haunting of the Rhine, when I
think of Cologne I think of the two flames in her,
Lorelei's, eyes, I think of her romantic curse the one
that Heinrich Heine sang her. Namely, she came to me
in my sickroom with a metre-long braid and laid it
onto my bed my bedstead, or gnawed lit. fir tree, in
the window ...... I'm strolling through Cologne on
the Rhine listening to the river rush, forgetting my
fate. Will language save me will poetry save us all
from the disaster of our time, before this substance ach
mild sky,

>Hölderlin says, 'the song may hardly disclose
>it,' he probably meant birdsong in the bur-
>geoning year, the whisper of lovers, *the hap-
>piness of the listener* who *listens* to the breath
>of the wind, the bringing forth of a strophe,
>etc. The ears, I mean, hearing is the relative
>of weeping the relative of those famous
>words of the philosopher Jacques Derrida's
>'are you going to speak to me of tears?'

how heavenly, mother said before her departure, my
eyes which can no longer read have received SUP-
PORT from my ears : that soul will be comforted,

composed between 4 and
20.2.18, *I saw it in
the twilight (namely)
heard it with these faun's
ears, ach*!

yes, Ely says, it has to do with passing water, no, Ely says, the
dead don't sleep. Spirits, namely, kneel down before the
machine go onto my knees, Brecht crying lectures on dialectic
(diadem), ach! Nerve-metamorphosis, title for a new book?
etc., thank you for the typescript, according to Ely, that your
texts arise through self-*propagating eyes*, this dream was a sum-
mery ROSINESS a lively rosiness, that I swung open the door
to the WC YES swung and could not recognize my own flat
any more could not remember it, but bathing box and lake
(which lake? was it that coldest of lakes alongside whose green
hem Ely sat, I mean, beneath the tall rustling tree and a lit. tis-
sue from out of his trousers a tip, namely, and slumped down
onto the MEADOW GREEN, whereas yng. mother my yng.
mother nestled herself down onto the meadow, and laughing
...... such snoring weather or weather conditions or *online-
winter*, I mean, this swung-open door to the WC),

> well back then Father would speak about hare
> sandwiches he'd brought me a hare sandwich
> it was something like, a hare's bread or for a
> hare, you had to take the bread in your arm,
> like a young animal, etc., when I was a child,
> namely, at the *forest's edge* (what a paradis-
> aical expression!), on tippytoes we dwelled /
> the honeyed eyes of the bees : berries, these
> immense doves and dove-spices, worm, it
> had to do with *sensations* = perceptions,
> according to Ely, that is, ancestors Slovenian
> ancestors, from Gottschee, according to Ely,

presumably why we've kept our black hair
into old age, *overkill*, etc.,

with a case of stage fright a case of scrap fright at the half-open
vis-à-vis window courtyard-window = cockiness-window I
caught, peeped a weeping red watering can, green meadow-
button

it looks like purple fruit!

buzzword 'nature-writing', I find myself in a
psychical state-of-emergency, weeping, with
the ship the package = paletot, the package
came with the ship, its husk was wet, I mean,
the package came with the ship came across
the sea, came with the ship across the sea,
came with the ship, with the *lit. ship*, with the
lit. paper ship, according to Ely. Came across
the beloved (sea), when only just red,

morning's, she'd already pulled on *her swimsuit*! then, in her
swimsuit, despite the cold, into the sea despite the cold she took
a swim in the sea, I mean, beside all the fish, she saw a ship.
Presumably as a child in blue garb, was sick to my stomach but
had to know a sentence by heart *recite*! *sweetly*! *sweetly*! *as a
child*! tumbled into the school garden's pond, as a child! the
ragged telephone, ragged tulip-hem,

hole-punch machine punching a LIT.
HEART instead of full moon, I wouldn't be

so destroyed if this urination, triumphant, *fury of snow*, etc., eagle of snow, tongue of snow, curtain of snow, body of snow, incessantly she-wolf, lit. cloud of snow, taste flakes of snow, fairy tales of snow, dream of a crystal ball in which it snows

ONTO A BAMBI!

dear Sarah, thank you for the lit. Testament smelling on yew : who's who of yew ......

my mother, hated card games,

24.2.18 ach desperate music of a Rossini,

or sheltered : a soft murmuring, by the time I arrived (late),
namely, Franz Schuh

are you : as me : from one moment to the next as well the
opening-of-the-eye words sentences erased to where did they
goodheavens submerged : went underground into deep forget-
ting and were still so wonderful like BLUDENZ, e.g., you say,
'do excuse me if I remain seated!', by the time I arrived you
were already sitting there, on the upholstered chairs and from
your mouth = bocca della verità = the truths sounded or I
could read them from your mouth, read them. Back then in
Rome when I laid my trembling hand into the bocca della
verità I did not suspect that decades later I would encounter
you, in the alcoves, ach the speech bubble from your mouth
'you love words head over heels with language', etc., I thought
of Jacques Derrida, asked you whether you loved him as much
as I, whereas this winter so triumphant, me there gone to seed,
SHELTERED my parents up to their ends ...... bent forward
in a gust of wind. The jaybirds the vanities that please us so,
you say, or greened with a hand-of-palm it's sickleing, the
night, you were a touch melancholic, look it's growing on you
the philosophy of truth from the heart ('it was all about feel-
ings' = es geht nur um Gefühle about ghostlylandscapes
ENGADIN), 'union suit', 'hot-water bottle', *Pink Torso* by
Rachel Whiteread,

your name on the street walking or freezing your
name favourite vein,

1.3.18, I
mean :

someone asks me about the subject, namely, *tow-line* of the new book, I say 'don't lose hope!' and look out onto the winter sea, it's about NOTHING and it's about EVERYTHING, perhaps polyphonic, it's about sensations = I mean, perceptions, in the sense of matter : table of matter, it's about bad blood : blue blood or lifeblood : ach about a lng. life it's about the bang the bang of infatuation, futilities, fantasies daydreams or how EvS whispers 'to bury one's head in the morning, that is, in the first morning light onto the kitchen table and very first tears, then FANTASTICAL!' ...... so, with a thousand arms enticing language something like tempting, shoulder to shoulder,

> this excessive, BAMBI-NATURE : ha!ha! childhood's classics, SLANGE, you say, SLANGE! You try to hiss, the hiss of a snake, back then out on the narrow footbridge, sunning itself I've forgotten the place I forget the place / the name of the place has *slipped* my mind indeed simply fallen from my forehead, ach pink mallow forehead your forehead, your eternal forehead,

that turning open the sink, I hear a voice saying to me: 'you're lovage a fleet of wild daffodil.'

The lit. wood's TYRE!

Fleet of narcissus, narcotic narcissus, at a lake (in a name in the neck in the bark in the night etc., crossing a lake, a hand in the

water, diving, the eye's waters, you shield : screen, this SUN-
WHEEL, namely)

2.3.18, once again find
the collected poems
of Höld. 'we would
like to separate' ......
in your, nymphgarden,

'this dog, howling storm, this all-too-make-up, you know, namely, red evening sky, have done penance for evil deeds : a whole life long evil deeds : immense evil blood, etc., in a morning dew in a hall : in a *hall of anemones* in a *nymph garden*! this abstract mode of writing, you know, whoever early in the day, I mean, nodded off : *nodded off once again*, that a sketch = lit. miss sketch : drawing oneself, that is, nodded off over and over (when writing a letter, well, such enigmatic broom = genet (Fr.), something like the Neckarhalde road in a white robe, etc.), when I read Konrad Bayer for the 1. time, I said *no I don't get it*!

I mean, this dog's forehead

immeasurable tuberose, August's haunt so that even his spit, crouched, I was cloned at 30!, ach rosehip-delirium, my green eye stares into the glaring midday light, the red berries the berries currants how they shine, Jacob Marrell's *Still-Life with Flowers* on a tabletop, you knock with lit. hearts, voice in your breast, decoration : white butterfly Hölderlin, at the stem of the glass with a handle, namely, watercolour of bitter orange! On the lit. table something of rain, Seville orange, Palermo ...... I mean, she paints : Martha Jungwirth paints bitter orange rain, deep pink : a groaning deep orange : unnameable deep pink, Martha Jungwirth, her yearlong tears, well yeah, I say, such white moths in a fever month, in a glass, that is, while fishing while taking one's temperature that ...... not being able to hear any more! so variable, you say, a time in which one

TAKES CARE OF one's friends, another time in which one
does not, as soon as possible a deafness of time, ach astutter in
the mornings, when I was a boy : ossified often I'd sprained
my left foot, interchanged my feet, in the monastery garden I'd
like, AND FLOX! *when I was a youngster!* When I raved!

> Snarling in the air! My brother was a wax
> candle, she wanted = Brigitte S. = with her
> cat = cavalier = through the fields and
> maple-world, etc.

namely, one goes away on foot, in hospital opened the door to
sleep therapy with an elbow real quiet in the hallway too, I
mean, death one spoonful at a time : ghastly bug!

> this enchanted lit. note, these adverbs scattered in all
> directions : a system of WELL-LOVED!,
> I mean, crumpled : the soul crumpled, the soul, like a
> patent-leather shoe! (crumpled),

who said 'so secretly (so) Matisse there the curtains overflowing
onto the table, with flowers, apple, who said the garden is
abloom : such feathers-of-air (a real smacker), that is, shattered
snowdrop,

> *the moment she showed off her 18-year-old pussy!* '

on the gates the sparrows the 3 red currants thanks to which I
realized that the painting was from a previous century, namely,
by Jacob Marrell 1613/14 with yellow tulips, on a tabletop,
young quince, namely, the interior of an image, supernatural,
you say, supernatural cold!

giggling most of the way as we through the endless
woods, how yng. we were, in these trout-hills

the turban's bandeau—

HOW I DRAG MYSELF OVER,

Haarlock's repetitions

4.3.18, gradually,
I wiped : I smeared
beloved's speech,

Jean Paul's lit. blue TINT, the trunk of your writing, the idea comes closer that between the rosebushes you, in the pub's courtyard ('Margareta') pitter-pattered and that lent me wings, indeed in your beautiful handwritten letter your forgot to close the parenthesis with which you opened the letter at the end : I can feel the draught I can feel it. At the end of the 1. page you used a dainty lit. sign (ə/ə) : it looks like a pair of eyes with a strong nose and seems to be whispering the challenge 'please turn around!', I mean, it was *a glamour*,

I'm going to the kitchen to eat breakfast! I call out, *the catafalque* at the end of the garden (where we still have never sat), veiled in black cloths, it was already getting dark, etc., Aurélie Le Née called that you a faerie, ach the twofold experience, of a meadow, of a lit. tint, namely, lit. tint ...... I was wearing a black plate cap,

such an angel-like paper plate, you say, there was a lit. tray made of porcelain in Café Sperl! which COMPLETED! me euphorically before to the reading I, I say 'it's remarkable where all our passions *hound* us!'   like

sleeveless this church!

a rapture, you say, an overdose of nature, you say, magnificent bloom bleeding out, this contemplation : rumination in the early morning deep and cindered and sprawling across the kitchen table, I mean, like the mother of God *the food service at 9*!, we want to SAP AWAY, you say,

as if tracing my left brow, eyebrow or stud, with a dark
lit. branch, you, you know, I'm afraid of dying desti-
tute. How, dark ear, *Fürchtegott*, well, my dotted brow
eyebrow, had fallen IN LOVE with the fringes : blue
fringes of a *corn cockle*, that one rooted with the grop-
ing, or something like that, the dead one's steps,

fnufffnuff, fnufffnuff,

13.3.18, let us
go out! Like candles!,

you said 'roof or plateau' the roof awning ALBERTINA cap =
temple of art, curry like a cleaning rag on the sideboard = cre-
denza : imploring yellow on the windowsill, radishes and straw-
berries : stormy red on the field bed, I'm perched on my field
bed and sketching a bouquet of speech, namely, recognize that
these bushes of speech sent out a scent, I mean : in tears I learnt
that this *sleeveless* feeling of happiness. Well presumably there
was a connection between the generations of colours and all the
horns on the country inn's walls ...... in the morning nausea
upon seeing the colour violet in a lit. dish whereas you before
me with pale skin etc., back then with your lit. dog you *staged*
an exchange of glances, which of the two of you : which of the
two of you could hold the other's glance longer : stand it,

> liverwort up-slope I mean on the meadow :
> going up the stairs I mean liverwort going up
> the stairs in blue on a green meadow,

you write you write me, overnight overnight you grew pigtails
or horns, you write 'I woke up and started because on my head
I'd grown horns or a braid, etc.,' the horrible things, you say,
happen AT NIGHT, you know, you wake up and a horn or
braid on your forehead, I hate turbans FOOTBALL TOO
(namely, football!), you went out of the house, citing 'oh
Sirocco take me up with your tongue!', turtle agency, I dreamt,
snuffsnuff in a beautifully situated psychiatric ward, wow!

> how I drag myself over! rosy cock cry, Cy Twombly's
> art, e.g., every summer I missed the opportunity the

jasmine in the park ach it stirred up my chest. Whereas the burning cats in Rome, dripping yes! wisteria dripping from the balustrades, lit. tint of violet wisteria rapture, you know …… sprawling out across the kitchen table, back then I had the black plate-cap on : *that did not clothe me* : *listen*! : *that did not clothe me*, such Bengali woods, such speech-work

WILD *and* CONCRETE (dear Sarah thank you for the lit. wooden table with yew and elite, and scribbles), wow! lit. pale-green cloud! wow!

> 16.3.18, while
> letter-writing
> dozed off!

to Martha Jungwirth,

this straddling in the a.m., this word's been following me, in
the a.m., perhaps a word from a translated language, you say,
from a field of carnations, perhaps *that light-green thing* : light-
green phantom, I mean, phantom of spring, of a spring por-
trayed with lit. points of green and pink, loosely bundled
together with a cord of bast, etc., any light-green thing in the
dawn in the twilight of a memory whereas Martha Jungwirth's
mallow colours, the doleful lit. bouquet, *doleful heath-dog vio-
let*, voiced passion, etc., I was enflamed, etc.,

> namely, the wood butterfly. We are the rain's
> baptized, exchanged clothes like playing
> children ...... narcissus-shouldered, corn
> cockles and gladioli,

sometimes instead of the words which have escaped me a Dio-
tima of hot tears, for I did not know that much siskin : strands
of hair DAUB over the left eye, back then in D. : *lit. basket with
claws*,

> it was a corn poppy it was a *lit. tint of painting*,
> I'd fallen into a delirium

the food service comes at 9

> 19.3.18 I, swallowed
> it down : your
> hands your hands :
> *they were asleep*

65

' •/. this symbol', I mean, paralysed sun the moun-
tain air in this *alley* : 'vägen' in Swedish? ach, this
question mark : cavalier with a cravat! that I, a water-
carrier plunge my feet into hot water, that I wiped
smudged my favourite language—why? perhaps I am
living in an alleyway. Having to do with language a
wonderful language.

A lit. bit of father : *Papa*! Father's constitution : *Papas*! Papa
chauffeured, summers we drove to D., through the lanes, the
wild lanes I remembered GREEN, childhood's variety, back
then flitting : coughing, at night coughing in the country house,
lovely moon in the roof window, that the old photos *revealed*
to me : how back then all of 9 years old together with my
schoolmates I would turn left or right, it was in springtime it
was in the school garden there were lit. spoons, *so endogenous*,
I was waiting for him, kissing me, to open my lips but it was
more like he pressed a kind of STAMP upon them ......
namely, exciting : asked myself what kind of bird what kind of
blooms what kind of climes = feelings I'd be presented with,
etc. One sleepless night I stood at the window and saw that a
torch *a featherbed* in the vis-à-vis building had burst into flames
and I was afraid of us being wiped out by fire, as well as
defeated, in the a.m., in any event.

> Ach the summer as the summer how the summer flit
> past and I too flit past, ach the dove how it flits past,
> ach the snowy air, you say, flit past. I mean, back then,
> in the vanished years, you say, the fears of hell,

ach the tedious time of year, and looked into the valley *into the sepia-coloured*, do you remember, a tuft of dreams, you were going down the stairs, Duchamp's nude descending a staircase

dumbfounded lit. window,

that the tufts of flowers that the mimosas that the mimosa bushes on their tippytoes (scampering) that these molten birds that the *colourful Rhine*, etc., that adjectives bring colour to a text, you say, that a swallowtailed watch brings colour to a shaman's robes, that your lit. crimson chalice,

'you're so lousy!' (adj.),

24.3.18, flickering
foot. My
pocket calendar LIES!

everything APPLIED, SMEARED with green felt-tip pen :
credenza shopping net lit. streams through the kitchen—oh!
on the kitchen floor the lit. amount of silhouette : the silhouette
of a bird with unlocked beak = indeed it's spring! ach how he
loved to eat Osterpinzen!, palm sundays these storms raging!
ach how the lit. springs bubbled : wheezed in lovely lines,
declaiming throughout the kitchen too (spelling out
DÖBLING), the perspective of the mountains along the hori-
zon, a heap of apples and applications of the rosary,

> at the earliest shouldering branches of pussy
> willow! all-too-blue sky's habit tied-down,
> yellow tulip-habit but spears. Of flower petals
> (sweet as a painting of that Fauvism!) the
> ancient Chinese already warning about *bad
> air*, etc.,

ach your angelic! and angelic paper plates, and how they slept
how your hands slept! my basic word is NO! NO! and NO!,
am I a ragged bird am I decay?

> paper plate's delicate language, you say,
> whereas all of 8-years-old, played *Diabolo*,
> you say (these spears of flowers), these spears
> how they pierce me, I mean, of spring,

25.3.18

through the whitish crack, of the curtains : wintry cuddle a bit
sooty the window cushion, back then, in the living room
against winter's discontent, you know, I'd lean against the win-
dowsill, for my own sake the *shape of a sow*! namely, poured
tea (whereas the ANTS across the breakfast table, etc.,), I
mean, played around Robert Schumann's mouth. I mean, a
smile would play around Robert Schumann's mouth whenever
he listened to Mendelssohn-Bartholdy's music, ach one's
favourite kisses in the mouth. It just so happened that a puddle
of breakfast tea, poured out over the tabletop ...... with bits
of mandarin in my mouth I couldn't articulate, a bit fever-
pitched! Easter bells on the trip to Rome, godly cleaning rag,
linen on carmine red blinds pulled down to LOCK OUT the
light, genital wavelength we haven't seen each other in a long
time so covered-in-leaves,—

> over and over $=$ *de novo* : Abraham : they sur-
> face in memories : your feet in the lit. river of
> D., etc., you say it has to do with perception,
> were sitting on the street by the Chinese cov-
> ered-in-leaves, listen, strangled times bad-
> tempered March! ask if you'll go to the sea,
> Croatia's, I ask you, I walked into your arms!

Adagio, you.

> 27.3.18, Café
> Griensteidl is no more

Café Griensteidl, Café
Griensteidl now is
Café Klimt

it excites me for a long time (with torn limbs), so that under a clear-blue sky ecstatic, it excites me ecstatically, I mean, this painting, etc., for 3 days now I have been lying folded limbs (see above) across this wonderful PAINTING which teaches and enriches me—would I have preferred to become a painter perhaps? pointing the way, like Ponge, I remember the points of sparrows nesting in the bushes ...... back then in Bad Schönau did (I) buy myself, NO, a painted cup of Bad Schönau, whereas I'm sitting in front of my Alpen window, *or dissonant*, lit. green leaf, *of wax*! : strange, like a dish, of marzipan, March-cold : Lenaublues, maybe (I) had stepped onto a natural wave, a wave of Gosau Lake's, a lit. coniferous forest in Rohrmoos God only knows how I stepped into a lit. coniferous forest in Rohrmoos, my foot slipped on the spruce-needled earth, rushed to the lit. town, isn't that so, angel-like, namely, a joint, before my feet I see the green wax : fantasy,

> Robert Schumann's smile played, *or played around his lips*, whenever he listens, listened, to Felix Mendelssohn Bartholdy's music, that is, covered-in-leaves,

I listened I listened to this lit. spruce forest in front of me I see the language : the language of painting, I raved I raved about the lit. spruce forest, but now I MUST CHANGE THIS TONE AT ONCE! :

> this snow-almanac just won't quit, I mean, wheezing, these Easter bells which have flown to Rome, wheezing

on their way to Rome, ere they hurled past the flaming palms in Währinger Strasze,

can you (get) me *a powder puff*, I mean, *the moon's a powder puff*? ach on the corner where it (had) snowed and Linde W. let me in to her *blood-red* car (where we reclined rather than sat), whereas the blank blooms in my head, etc., presumably eye-water : eye-water ...... *what have I done to hurt you?*, still want a CHIMAERA : ach I want to write one lit. page more.

In your tumultuous letter ach the mountain flew away like a bird, I had not, namely, dunked consecrated blessed my ankles / in rosé / that source of the Danube in Donaueschingen, that is, BRILLIANT in the setting sun's last rays,

back then were we really in Marathon on the coast because I wanted to be close to you, but as you moved away my tears began to roll, *into the sea*,

VERDIGRIS IN D., I say,

29.3.18, I was sitting next to you and you said you had it in mind: minimal sign of language = Peter Waterhouse, angel-like, namely, a joint, woe betide if a snake-like S, *namely*, *beloved lit. snake*, marches in between 'angel' and 'like', that god's mercy, once he said '*shadow bag*', once he said 'charming kitchen!', once he said 'winter so spangled!' or my left foot was denied! or deaf! or dew! in the upper-lefthand corner of your letter the lit. word DEW, were you thinking of a lit. drop of dew, I mean, upon

a green kissed blade of grass a drop of dew, the half-cloud of a dove a dove's red feet, I wrote

> I stubbed it the lit. red shoe stubbed over it beneath a full moon, really, a full moon, I was standing at the window, it ATTRACTED me!

I had a hooded eye sky-blue hooded eye, real small in the corner a completely scribbled over. Piece of paper crouching a lit. boot, screaming lit. boot, I'm drawing a lot, Easter today today is Easter Sunday, you say, may Easter Sunday come many a time more, I'd like it now and for ever evermore. Leafing through my life's pages, *tallow* of pain immense cheeks and tears, in the language of my feralization, etc., back then in Linz, on Pöstlingberg hill your loving way of handling lit. flowers YELLOW the ones I picked for you I think, you were sitting with them in your hand, looking at yellow flowers, the way you caressed the yellow flowers, their face, I mean, as you deny me such a caress, a green *blade or throat*, of a hymn, that was enough for me, back then, sitting my your side, Pöstlingberg, that night glimpsed the *tiniest splinter* such a sparkling twinkling splinter of moon, such a Kleist-immortelle,

1.4.18

sitting at a worm-eaten. Table outside last summer why did that word, the beak of a bird on parquet, these thin, I mean, my lit. stems. A boundless meadow, I mean, broken snowdrop with white shards in the grass so that I had to weep that the wren's song, we often sat out in the garden, listening to these, *carnation pages* ...... these thin, I mean, lit. sails, from afar (from out of the window) down the hills the storm birds of spring, you wanted a pair of WHEEZING snowdrops beneath the stairs,

to adore me ...... ach, this linnet this flaneur! I've lost, namely, the lit. pine. Somewhere in my flat. Falling I surrender, in falling I surrender, surrender to the fall : to the pain!

such a blackbird such a black bird with an unlocked beak : tin bird : you could see where you could open it up, sunken eye, a kid brother? with artificial white tail feathers? but only one foot, how now. Breadcrumbs in an open beak whereas writing these lines my heart's on a hop my heart ticks and trumpets, a lit. bird lying on the left cheek the lit. bird singing a cantata! lit. bird cowering *in the browser*—what's a browser? sometimes my parents would go play skittles but I was still small ...... did the illustrious composer come towards me *swinging his cane* because I'd forgotten my walking stick in the hills, in fact in your letter from 10.3.18 you forgot to close the parenthesis with which you opened the letter at the end, I mean, at the end of 1. page you wrote a delicate symbol :

expressing the prompt to 'please turn over'. While opening, the faucet, I hear you whisper 'the wood's tyre', 'lovage', 'wild daffodil', 'eye-water', someone asks me about the material of my new book,

      ach a carnation page ...... you've scratched your arm bloody, red blooms have sprouted along your arm

                4.4.18, Mother before
                her departure would repeat
                whatever I said

until you went mad on me : my melodic style, *picking* a lit. piece of paper *up* off the floor PICKING UP a lit. piece of paper covered with notes, as if I were picking up : purple blooms which onto a meadow, had floated down, rather melodramatic this glittering glances glittering tears, an image of Samuel Rachel, tottering, the image's title *Lily's Satchel*, you could only see her feet and her hand holding onto it ...... I picked a lit. piece of written paper up off the floor, off a meadow picked up fallen tree blossoms, etc., hallucinations in the a.m. : I always saw people walking about the garden, etc., my face's or spirit's decay, lemon-morning! You say, lemon-morning! breath of liverwort, lit. wood April sweet April a tiny mimosa bouquet on the kitchen floor, it's 8 April 2018, I schlepped myself to Café Eiles I thought the most important thing in my life was that someone taught me how to read and write, back then it was raining onto the bushes in the school garden, unforgettable time I was a lit. girl with black hair and blue eyes. *I met you in the woods the strangest in branches,* Great-Grandfather was a forester,

the eagles will be the last creatures alive, in your Burberry. In your Burberry you look like you've just come from New York, my Botero! I'm in pain, a terrible dream, you say, it overshadows my morning, what a terrible dream a new moon over the 'Albertina's' roof, ach pale rippling new moon, ach rippling half-face, I've always been so half-hearted,

have bitten the tip of my tongue 2 days in a row now, while
eating breakfast, cut my finger too on drawing paper,

                              7.4.18, what's a
                              poem allowed to do, you
                              ask, can it do everything,
                              puddle of tears ......

I mean, like parrots what's that all about then, in yearning veil of rain (with parrots), what's that all about then, what subject should I research, no, she says, dignified ideas-for-words spirited spectres, you don't need to research a thing, ach parrots! sweet April! süszer April, I say, *or Botero!*, he appeared, literally from out of nowhere!, and I wonder why Botero of all people, his lit. mouth tiny pink mouth IN THE MIDDLE OF A MOON FACE, etc., I fell in love with this lit. mouth : pink bud of a lit. mouth, I fell in love with his : Botero's, dissonances, what's this all about then, with parrots? I want to *unlock* : kiss his lit. mouth : lit. garden of Eden, embrace it with hidden tongues,

> art is my everything. Exhibit words as words, without unfolding their meaning, I call Ulla-Mae, how spring has awoken, a completely yellow mandarin, sleep's shoes, the lit. crown, Botero's lit. mouth, something parrot-like pulsing on your shoulder, etc.,

your foliage, namely, a leopard mantle upon awaking, on my bed, the flowered umbels wavered in the window, to paint in pink, on pink blotting paper, so much Beethoven ...... the sum of all tears, a blue sword in your left eye, I think RED, like Botero's lit. mouth,

> ach, page-throng (parrot)

> 15.4.18, *so waterproof!*,

MOTTO

at the forest's edge, there, houses ablaze at dawn ach puff at
your beak shoes! As the paintbrush whipped out of your hand
(Dali painted Gala with a cutlet on her shoulder) the last days
of May Danubewards, you know, on a yellowed, photograph,
we're standing in front of some floral wallpaper, are you wear-
ing a yellow BODY?, an erring of sunflowers,

17.4.18

I'd like it a bit WINDY in kurrent script, I wanted, delicate blackbird, to sit with you at a table in the wind as no one else (dear me, there) etc., is flying : you start : to scream and I melt, like *Bride of the Wind* (when someone smiles at me, across the bridge), how I melt melt thither, and flew, out of the window niche, the cloverleafs screamed too, crawled with me into the green, ach those verses nodding into the water!, summer last so glowing, was, that feverish, unlocked, beaks (of clover) *meanwhile rosette of May*, etc., the Christmas tree! Christendom! on the pasting table where the cloverleafs, shoot forth, imploring bushes, you know, Botero's tiny lit. mouth, pagethrong upon your shoulder, verse! : aping, ornament of afternoon sun, collage of flowers in your letter, I say, a pale lit. bird flew to me a crimson ROBIN, *pick up*! picking a lit. piece of paper up off the floor, listen : written lit. piece of paper, as if I picked up pink blossoms, recently, I say, the feminization of the language, but I was small, Chagall's *The Walk*, mother before her departure would repeat whatever I said, where would her urgent and numerous UNCEASING prayers (have remained)

      I'd left my likeness behind, I'd like a lit. Venice (windy) ......

                                    23.4.18, before I left the
                                    bed : *buzzing*
                                    speech, with
                                    torn-open, eyes,

sensualized, I mean, sensualized, what gives me wings, I say, my friends grew old with me I grew old together with my friends. In point of fact, we're hares : flying hares with crop and shrub, isn't that so, take a step into the garden, the rosettes of spring flowers, a drop of dew upon your forehead, 2 minutes on your right ear. Slumbered or fluttered, in half an hour I'll start *to buzz*, that she in her Alps there that she (Mama) over and over in her Alps, so something (more or less) like cherries, a spell : a tree in pink, EvS lecturing on the phenomenon of 'stuffed animals' ...... the seasons are edging into one another, there were these fields of lilies behind the provincial railway station, was that in St Pölten or Tulln? no, but it sure smelt nice!

> the mountain air in this alley, back then on the wooden bridge in D., as we bent down over the lit. stream : molten birds, you pointed at some fish. Ach darting fish their scale-studded gowns, I mean, you called out 'food!' and 'feast!' colourful RHINE, etc., my daily planner is lying. I'd like to *leaf*! through my favourite books! I'd like to trip through my favourite woods, he familiarized me with Marc Chagall's work, he swung me through the air, like BELLA.

That the yng. moon was flickering, I say, with a halo, I say, this lit. mouth this tiny *Botero*, this PARROT-throng upon your shoulder (she asked, 'Why parrot? because of the colour?', 'no', I say, 'it's just the word! the word *parrot!*') back then Mama painted a divine parrot for me in my exercise book ...... perhaps just to manifest her love, I mean, of painting, like blood the colours overwhelmed everything, like Botero! a parrot-throng, I didn't mean the parrot I said but *the word!*, I'd fallen in love with the love affairs of his, Botero's, pictures, I'd wandered like a ghost : one lit. ghost after another (Tom Waits on posters downtown, or 'Tom waits for you', etc.), Schiller in Fr., the Fr. word 'joli' so sweet, it's following me,

> while sprawled out, on my old bed and *dozing off* : dozing off for 5 seconds, I mean, the glimpse of this shattered winter rose, the wind seemed to be blowing my immortal (soul)!, all kinds, back then, (the lovely) school garden, green pleats, etc.,

> 26.4.18, he always arrived with a *lit.*
> *letter* ......

the large black bird flies through the rain, the white hare with crop flies over the grass, Sakai Hōitsu, the roebucks are coughing the cat is crying! = in the Japanese tongue,

...... you were painting drops ach dabs of spring, I see green, spring's sash back then in D., was a child was I a child, in the sand ach in the *handcart*! drunk-on-peonies, etc., handful of blueberries, so, I see, above the back of the kitchen stool, this violet, I mean, lit. sky, painted with birds of paradise, etc., night is a stranger you know, dear Titzi dear lavender (Madrid blinds ha!) tear-pale Madrid, etc., there's a rage in me a roaring tongue pleated cheek, roaring *and full of art*, Sarah Kirsch, standing before the shard-heap of my life, 'the

women with yellow hair' Picasso-like, on the kitchen table peonies and hydrangeas, you're like the ECHO of a breath, the clematis' furious clothes in the front garden of the estate in D., all of a sudden something stops (correspondence, e.g.), so transfigured violet apostrophe of a cat, I let all hope go ...... breath of liverwort,

when I woke you up a few days ago at 3 in the morning (in a storm) you spoke like a dove speaks. He said it's a love story, on my right side I am full of blood,

ach you, cobalt-blue feathers, you were, namely, a bird and
spreading your wings ......

(into the grave astraddle),

6.5.18, had brilliant, in
the melting
sun. And Linde W.
let me in to her red
car! where we reclined
more than sat, back then I
was carrying,
namely, the barstool
into her
summer flat, HOW
SHE'D HUNT!,

In a box the extreme tears, of a rabbit fur, as legendary as a summer night, a bit of angelica in a garden, boundless the wilted hortensia flower in the glass, I mean, common siskin in my bed, the nurse laid her long braid onto my bed or box bed, those nights you with your *ROBIN*! THE BRIGHT BLOOD IN YOUR ROBIN, being so still the evening made me think of your braid upon my box bed, I will strangle myself with your long braid, the meadow red, a chimaera, ach I want to write another lit. page how is it I made you sad, I'll be at yours around 13.15, I am so byzantine, at 13.15 at yours, ach this green, spring's sash, you speak like a dove speaks, we found you again in the lanes, back then in my early years with PAPA to D., through all the lanes, like a lit. dog and *principally*, caught my hand in the car door, how I cried, how Mama froze. I mean, along the Loire mostly along the wings of my nose I wore the pearls as I sat there on the banks of the Loire, I dreamt something or other I dreamt something or other something repugnant though in the ALBERTINA's Hall of the Muses and the muses were greeting me, though the clothes! of the clematis deep blue, namely, night's descent in the garden at Ischl, etc.,

I scurried, namely, scurried was out of my senses was indeed out of my senses, cilia-flight, my hand almost torn off in the car door how I shrieked, I remember : he was so fuming crying (my god!) ...... you were perplexed, you were prophetic, you knew that something bad would happen! something bad would happen to us! (Martha was chubby but

so becoming = dressed in a lit. skirt, so that
we, so blue admired her), back then I did
everything I could to get myself a Fr. bed, do
you remember the Fr. bed stood then next to
the *fire-spitting stove*!, I secretly ask myself :
what did I dream of doing with a Fr. bed,

well, anyway, I'd fallen in love with the blue! *fringed*! petals of
a CORN COCKLE, I dreamt of a really sm. grave (a child's
grave?) with glowing red flowers—though it is common to
adorn a child's grave with white ones, *or blood*

8.5.18, I saw how he
showered her SKULL!
with kisses,
namely, so small, namely,
so wonderfully small

I mean, the myrrh, dear lavender = fantasia of Madrid, tear-pale : so small, namely, *so wonderfully small*! so small veins! so favourite scent! as if you ('framed') with a dark lit. branch (*picked up* off the ground!) you sketched my left eyebrow POOR AS A BEGGAR above the left eye, you know, I mean, that a dark ear of grain dotted my left eyebrow, in that the lit. barking, bells of St Thekla, as they say 'the 3-o-clock-bells are ringing for a funeral' (I explained to him how I write : as if I a handful of marbles, in the sand, etc.), I mean, lit. light-green watering can with pointed tongue!,

> the one time with the green watering can in the garden in D. at dusk : *screaming* striding between the flowerbeds SPLASHING, namely, like eyes SPLASHING = tears SPLASHING as a child, the other time as a novice in the hospital garden 2 years ago, with bonnet of early evening, you know,

this clog decoration no grey umbels of clouds *by Botero*, in the enbushed! the dentist's waiting room solemn sibling pair, painted by Botero

such giggling dumplings, I say,

early this morning *lax*! but happy as I heard Alban Berg's *Altenberg Liedern* ...... I mean, headlines : half headlines from Cadiz = half pre-historic work see below :

('heartfelt', Robert Schumann writes 'heartfelt',
......)

9.5.18, Alban Berg, *5*
Orchestral Songs after
Postcard Texts
By Peter Altenberg op.4,
(beyond the borders of space)

for Otto Breicha, approximately,

he'd *flirted*! flirted with a lit. volume, then flirted to her lips isn't that so, and everything revolved around his lit. collection of soul that is day and night at her heart taken up so MISTRAL and said 'I'm so attached to you how attached to you I am', he says 'my heart's so taken this blue heart of mine god defiant heart god pale heart *blind*!' : recognized me by my foot by my step and as the sun sank : *the Verdigris sun sank*!

    the tiniest dawdling, namely

I caught a glimpse of you! adorably caught a glimpse! like coocoo, like Botero! ach such a beautiful day with you, with Botero's lit. cloud, puffy sibling pair! on Botero's sofa, I'd like to take a walk in this meadow, with Botero,

        this blue pincushion *ablaze*, so Marcel B., a Romantic
        method,

                10.5.18, I mean
                'combine!' that I've
                striven for so long in
                my work
                to combine avant-gardism
                with classicism! ...... so
                dabbed at!
                how I dabbed! ......
                I mean, HANDROD!
                (so, over the back of the
                kitchen stool), etc.,

lissome month of May, your letters scold me, they scold me about this and that, back then in D., lit. basket with burdocks, namely, slung me, namely, wild as boys, slung me wildly so that in my curls that in my curls the wild burdocks ach opium blade ach baby's breath how the boys slung me wild how midnights I would over the edge of the balcony and see a throng of favourites : favourite stars, so stunning so stunned a throng of favourites = painters : de Chirico, namely : his lit. foot bells, namely ...... are the stars then the sky's PAGES? a sky's : a sky's *paintings?* these traces of sopranos? on my tippytoes I am invisible, the food service, today at 10, in an hour of the morning, tear for tear across my cheek : enormous cheek, of a red apple, the swallow's head weeps, back then you waved at me for a long time you were a swallow and waved at me for a long time with your wings (is it a swallows' wedding is it a flirt is it a wedding of tears is it a love-story?), it's a rage within me a wistfulness

> so profound I saw you in the form of a swal-
> low above the Vltava dear Doctor, here the
> bones here the buds of my footprints I cannot
> tell IF BROKEN?

I'm broken in body and soul, your patient, I saw you in the form of a *raven* above the Vltava! in the early morning the fishermen in their boats there. In the rain in the rain the cross-eyed window from vis-à-vis, I'm painted like so, in the snowy, May, in the snowy grove, ach Alpenedge! in a snowy May (every word a single scar, etc.),

you're bent over the lit. spot of grass, whereas
the halls, of my eyes, how spring is like a
mandolin how the liverwort teems beneath
lawn chairs how I blazed, you know, I say to
L.U. while we were crouched in the lit. fir-
tree forest, yeah! you looked like Gertrude
Stein you did, so combed back, as if living in
a lane (of language) ......

18.5.18, I let
her fall crying :
fall! I mean, the
narcissus : then there at the
edge of the woods. Finally :
finally changed my clothes,
just as kids

a sugar cube beneath the kitchen stool, *fevered*! or swept up!
ach Dante Alighieri is holding up an open book in his left hand,
I mean, spangled forehead! indeed wool stockings : lit. island
enchantingly clear bushes (your hands your hands : they slept),

> as if I had dreamt a lot as if I had dreamt illuminatingly
> in the drops of blood you shed at dawn the 29th of May
> I discover, it took place on a summer day in '94 sitting
> out in Leo Navratil's garden, we wore lovely straw
> hats to protect us from the sun (nevertheless our ears),
> reading Houellebecq to one another whereas Dante
> Alighieri offered to bring the flower arrangements we'd
> gathered in the garden (after the lawnmower had to
> death. Dragged them), to my home. But a number of lit.
> songbirds had hidden themselves inside, which I only
> noticed by their delicate songs), namely, for the shadows
> of the flowers had winged themselves. To death.

> I mean, the latest buzzword 'nature-writing',

> > 29.5.18, I'll charm the air
> > = ich werde die Lüfte
> > *schwärmen* ......
> > ach those were probably
> > shots in the
> > fragrant linden trees,

mental disturbance on 2 June 2018, a rustling in the early a.m.
a carpentering, this my beloved language, you know, snowfall
in June, something like a sky's bleeding-out, a sibyl, you know,
a stillness, had an epi-attack, a frenzy, had eye-feelings, loved
Rameau, I've drawn a few flowers : a few lit. flowers hushed
just so …… a snowflaked world in June as well, Egon Schiele's
Standing Girl with Hands Raised and harem trousers, ach pink
paw : orchids in the woods, *that hopping I!*, back then in
Rohrmoos, cowering in the woodshade of deer, such bee traffic
etc.,

> this industrious German-fever : German
> fever = Samuel Beckett's 'German Fever',
> namely, after a long deep sleep or shore. Of
> dreams. You say how this year has just raced
> by : from pasture-time to pasture-time, B.H.,
> when I awoke the sky was covered with grey,
> cloths and a pair of bees were buzzing in the
> window, sometimes these animals *dazed* (with
> boot-legs) as if they had *dipped* themselves
> into early summer, which with refined clouds,
> etc., with bee and breeze at the window, dear
> me! I mean, it was fairytale-like! and that the
> language was ENCHANTED, in this stock-
> still society of bees, you know, 'a throng (in
> one's socks)' in the estate, hateful to have to
> take care of some duties or other in the a.m.,

the comfort of a Klaus Reichert, I say, an old bee at the window
: right before the collapse! I mean, alternative bee, a collage of

doctors at the Evangelische Hospital, well, we were wandering within the white lilies' *shift*, tree-length studies, namely, for 3 weeks suffering from writer's block it really did cause me to break out in tears, whenever I walked past the lit. patch of woods on Hamburgerstrasze I thought of a production of a Beckett piece by the workshop of the avant-garde theatre there, towards evening a brimstone butterfly at the window, quite delicate, I am laying my heart at your feet,

30.5.18, *in the red rhubarb's shift,*

'you really played with fire! For Peter
Enzinger, and Georg Bernsteiner ...... '

the tapestry my mother wove with her bloody, bare, feet :
dragon and lions with people's faces, hydrants whereas, father
said come on we're going to look at the Zeppelin, one night
and tore me out of bed : above our heads a zeppelin it was prob-
ably a *cloud-sport*, etc., a winter's Inverness cape in the window,
I mean, a winter's Inverness cape. With blue rings : bags below
the eyes, in the window, New Year's elite,

to complain into, you say as that has settled
down onto a chair (丨丿)

in the a.m. perched on the side of the bed turned away from
the sun : a : a lit. bit of harp, in the ear, multiples in the front
garden of Café Sperl Georg Bernstein's eyebrows = a protec-
tive roof : *pm* over a tearing eye, something's swanned some-
thing's in mind I'm standing with my back to the wall, it was
probably a *cloud-sport*, etc.

31.5.18 Man Ray =
'Painted flatiron
and nails'
15.3 X 9 X 11.4 cm
(*Cadeau*)

you've really bossed me around, therein *the girls* grown and lost a white rose-parterre at one's feet = Jean Paul, blue and green coat like grass *cowered* on the kitchen stool, checked with lit. woods and wood ach with winds : Aeolian harp indeed annually, Aeolian harp of a storm powerful harp in the window across the way we'll burn! huge Aeolian harp of a storm in the window, I mean, in the Albertina's Hall of the Muses : GAIA's sweet brute whose name engraved, I've got to sleep a bit more ...... how the ravens in sleep, stilt my poems over to you,

> the settlements rumble down the slope, already gloaming I tore the endpaper of, a catalogue out in order to scribble hefty affair (rustling of the mice in the night etc.), *kin* in your skull. Horváth's death from falling = a tree's raving madness, reading misreading : we versify in that we misread, you push your headband onto your lit. skull, like a halo! heat all too heavy you've *planted* your headband like a halo, along your lit. skull, etc.,

ach this bush's siblings : brothers and sisters' lit. branch, I mean, understanding perceptions : my perceptions while taking a walk in Augarten Park, *in a loge of sun,*

> 2.6.18, this throbbing word COWL went underground early this morning, like heart,

it's more that he
pressed a, stamp
on my
lips so that
I never (wanted)
to open them again.

well yeah : purchased a really short lit. coat of faux fur (Ruben's lit. fur), behind yew hedge! Helene Fourment = shamefaced Venus, etc., it'll rain lit. monkeys!, for heaven's sake the lit. inkwell with its collar of blue ink (I mean, aperto), it must've been a year since you sat in my quarters, blonde sun nestling in your hair, Picasso called his painting *Woman with Yellow Hair*, uterus thwarted = no longer available, violet bulge of the lips blonde wig, rouged breasts ...... a bitten-into heart cherry bitten into at night, etc.,

> a joker of 3 green toes in the key of kitchen, ach azure : azzurro! back then that's how we went to the Adriatic Sea, that is, the sea flashing through the delicate landscape, I can sleep in the air,

soft smut!

After : *Stefan Fabi* naked

15.7.18

along the railway tracks back then with Mother, summers in Winterbach ...... whose wife was named Amalia and upon whose lifeless chest sat the lit. dog (Pauli) and attentive?, we anchored Gosau's lake = Grandmother's crop = digital crop, azure azzurro fragment of a Schottengasse, talent or trout. Go on, look : birthmark on the blanket, inverted commas, namely, Bad Ischl, in the middle of flowerbeds ('nature-writing' in the spa park, the day's post on my lap, etc., from 'cassette' EJ once wrote : meant uterus, change of colour : change of temperature my language when I Anglify it, isn't that so, lit. water fountain : my tears when I remember : glorious summer '18 : maybe the last one, decay when all's said and done, decay,

> as he Mahler's 5. I began to cry, but he said : 'don't cry!', the poet Stolterfoht steals 2 lines of mine. Summers in Bad Ischl in the leaves ...... (painting))

in the dental summer, shimmering source, hydrant. There were only 2 taxis in town, so that I didn't know : *a lack of language*!, whether it was called hummingbird or Constance, there's an unlucky star over town, in Papa's bureau = Francis Ponge : in Papa's cabinet heartfelt family photos. He'd come to visit me in the kitchen, and I pointed out some ravens to him on the roof across the way, Maria Lassnig's Iron Curtain *breakfast with ear* = thin and thick texture as juxtaposition of cluster and constellation,

Mozart Playing the Organ in Ybbs painting by Heinrich Lossow *c.* 1864, here the text for the intended book 'in the beginning was the glance' printed for you with a few observations on slow movement ...... met Alfred K. in Graz, he didn't know a thing about the Candlemas meeting, etc., a childhood memory of Leonardo da Vinci ...... : a sparrow in the bag a sparrow on the kitchen floor, a linocut showing Cup with Three Different Steams, you know, so that one wants to BLOW AWAY the heat at the same time, I was head-over-heels in. The Draschepark and in Waldmüllerpark too, the child's soul like the soft wind embracing the grass so that it took a bow, ach

this tune in the key of laundry, how often the day of one's death falls on the day of one's birth ...... your safety helmet planted into your skull = a sweet brute! (in the ALBERTINA's Hall of the Muses, where we sat) half-asleep : asleep-in-the-woods : Grandfather asleep-in-the-woods (as I sniffed about!)

Construction-Site Brain!

26.7.18, *ach how* the *world burns* ......

this visit's leaves in your garden. I stroked his cheek, more or less. Dürer's cheek. More or less, lit. brother in gold. At night however during the *blood moon's* splendour he began to die, we wept bitterly. The grave's stones railway tracks. Where have you gone? Such blue flower-death ...... *we love you*,

for EvS on her 62. birthday

29.7.18

in the surgeon's changing room or mossed-over mountain landscape = Barbara Frischmuth = who calls me and says crying. I mean, crying she pressed the *syncopations* of my latest books to her heart, well I did too. The sea of constructions : admired the grass the tops of the linden trees : I went to the changing-room window and said hello to the yew which had pressed itself, into the corner of the garden courtyard. In the frenzy of the yew, you say, that it was the first thing that struck you in this changing-room, etc., whereas the aquarium the shadowy slumbering. Hans Ulrich Obrist asked me for half a line : 'the virtue of the leaves', I hadn't grasped that the swallows had disappeared this 2. August—earlier than in summers past ...... Goya, yew and a lane of gingko trees, you say,

> I won't forget how we sat out in the garden of Bad Ischl *next to the burning* bush and listened to the swallows' hop and cheer *in the burning* bush,

half-asleep, I say, I see the line that I will write before me, *on 19. July there was a BLOOD MOON,*

8.8.18

in such a plum-grove ach! in such a plum-grove how they sat and drank in the shade of such a plum-grove. Eating from painted dishes (always take a book for LADY, etc.)

it is 11. August 2018, tropical temperature in a lit. case, fur-trimmed winter hood you say 'the SNW!', I mean, if that morning I'd wanted to sing a song (I confuse the point of view : for you and you, to you with you, you and you!) ...... if they'd taught me painting : Jacob van Ruisdael, e.g. *view of Haarlem with* bleaching *grounds* = The Bleaching Grounds near Haarlem, namely, on that morning : hand in hand so many years ago, mixed up the Muse of Sounds with the Muse of Colours : how the stream whispered next to our steps,

presumably it is still whispering today after so many years and the mornings there pre-sumably / still *pale, I mean, Wally.*

Back then in that mother-of-pearl summer still a lit. pale the morning was, I mean, as pale-as-tears = the tears were tears of happiness, we were young and *lovely* it was, namely, a really early morning in R., that we were hiking and the stream whispered next to our steps ......

the wild roses Mother loved so much : *beautiful syncopation*! beautiful Aesculapian

snake = lit. blue vein in the inner wrist there
where Mother tried to kill herself,

11.8.18, *for EJ*

'oh, come on!', so Beckett, dreamt the word 'gurgle', dreamt 'medical confidentiality', dreamt 'palette-winter', 'mossed-over parquet', August heat in D., but in the early a.m. your cold cheek, I mean, lit. marble table in the front garden ...... I've got to sleep a bit like the ravens asleep, STILTING past you my poems as in the distance (in summer) the settlements rumble (checked) down with lit. woods and winds the grasses at one's feet, last night luxurious dreams (expansive) in luxurious colours, drowning yew how green! at what hour, beneath what lit. hood the poet Robert Walser seemed old-fashioned to me or like objects on an old piece of furniture, etc., then he fell into the snow into a snowdrift and never got back up, whereas the Verdigris sun. We're burning up here, 37° today, ach your marble cheeks nights your marble cheeks (from Ponge) ...... she was proficient in the French = Elisabeth B., she said 'your manuscript isn't made of cardboard!', I visited her in her lavish first-floor flat (up creaking wood stairs),

> we've known each other for so long already we've
> known each other so many years, that you move about
> my life as if in a familiar place, you know,

eye-heat in D., August heat in D., half-asleep asleep-in-the-woods my great-grandfather asleep-in-the-woods, his rain-drenched cap!, on the kitchen table! a bitten-into heart cherry bitten into at night ...... stood to my right : *pearling*! the Muse Gaia, headband planted like a sweet brute! into your skull, I mean, in the ALBERTINA's Hall of the Muses where we sat, etc.

this sackcloth when it slipped out of his coat pocket my god he was sitting : sitting beneath the fir = lit. fir tree whereas in the distance Lake Atter!, rather platonic, I call out, *bushel of tears*, was head-over-heels in.

              15.8.18, I mean, the sky
              bleeding at 5 in the morning,
              (for weeks now have
              spent the glowing
              hot afternoon hours out
              in the garden of Café Sperl,
              crumpled
              paper, more or less),

this underbrush this photo the mountain air in this alley ......
in this photo I had the honour of standing in front of
COLOURFUL wallpaper : standing behind you in profile
whereas with slightly bowed head and arms crossed behind
your back you, I think, assessing or pensive, namely, musing
upon the lines : namely, reflecting upon the lines you'd written
for Hans Mayer : in which you shore his scalp with tailor's
shears (by the metre), I remember, for Hans Mayer's 90. birth-
day, etc.,

> that during a conference he, Hans Mayer,
> stood up and went to the open window,
> before he, came back,

I asked myself what the reason might have been why that turn
to the open window,

> which distracted me from continuing to listen
> to the speaker,

ach lit. bit of grass picked up off the kitchen stool, etc.

> I read 2 texts of Ilse Helbich's and shed tears,
> perhaps the texts had come from an *in-
> between*, I say, or they reminded me of
> Magritte's secrets, I mean, *over the carnations*!
> I was sitting there in the in-between (in front
> of the machine) ach overcome my vertigo,

well yeah : a really short lit. coat of ARTIFI-
CIAL LANGUAGE (Ruben's lit. fur), love
and glory, 'do you have any CONNEC-
TION to the Reichs Bridge?'

29.8.18

boundless lit. fountain you, feverish morning red you ......
you tell me that mornings you like to muse, how strange that
years ago a vision I. I was reading Marcel Beyer's BEE BABY.

> an unknown woman came up to me and said, I live in
> your flat now, namely, in the flat where you lived as a
> child (with your parents), as the unknown woman
> this revelation, *I soon began to tremble*, whereas the
> SPARROWS *shoeless* ...... you said 'a BUSHEL OF
> TEARS', I said 'Wedding / Berlin' (which means
> wedding), you said 'with 2 cracows', I said 'with
> chord and buckle', you said 'a keg of benumbment', I
> said 'I dreamt of walking!', as far as winter's IRON
> CURTAIN is concerned, I say, Maria Lassnig wrote
> 'Breakfast with Ear', etc.,

a *foot-angel* = like angel = Engel = that is, the word I incubated
during my 7 hours of sleep, it was something special for I was
trembling along the path through the woods whereas a lit.
woodland bird fluttered or lightninged against my forehead, I
mean, that I awoke with the word ARCADIA, *another time*
with the word Lettrism, I mean, how surprised the two neigh-
bours would be were, coming back from their holidays, they
to find the immense crimson GIFT! in front of the door to their
flat. I fidget across the tiled floor whereas *forever* in my fist my
shed, tears, got out of control, namely, *creeping* over me, ach!
how it *crept*! (in short : as a child), vague fears creep over me,

Martha Jungwirth writes 'Heavenly Father as Iron Curtain', as Wally's shadow in the woods, etc., my lit. sibling : the rain-soaked cap! : aroused my emotions,

with bee and breeze, at the window, dear me : in this society of bees, you know, namely, after a long deep sleep or beach or bouquet, over and over the word 'rhubarb' escapes me—but the stork feet before me,

1.9.18, slender,
rose garden sometimes,
dazed ...... in the
lilies' SHIFT,

scattered flower in the glass next to it the Christmas tree still decorated from last year, etc., but it's September '18, your brilliant awaking, your being-warm, in the body like blood or blushed cheeks, you're wisteria grape : dove you're hanging from the balcony back then Bad Ischl Hotel gold. Ship, namely, *tons of parents*,

> here a swing's a 'Hutsche' there a 'Schaukel',
> *I write proems*, you're a reformer a blue heath-
> dog violet pressing your destiny to my chest
> : a wooden frame out on the street to sit on
> with robins in the open air!, then internet-
> garden with half-naked READER in the
> front lawn which reminds me of a Monet, I
> mean, lit. coltsfoot woods got lost over there
> : my eye there, are you nuts? I keep dreaming
> of walking, ach *abyss of parents*, wool cap on
> the shelf, how the tears ach how our tears
> DELIGHT US

of the woodflowers! a grated chestnut leaf how lovely it smells! Fell asleep on the kitchen stool, the pencil fell out of my hand ...... with bee and breeze at the window, dear me! I mean, it was TREMENDOUS and that the language was an enchanted one,

> like a dangling language!

these toes like a keyboard! which I press down I plunk, *Piano*! says Mama, she brings me a Deleuze : an adoration, rucksack in the wind, I say, you even saw a lit. lilac there where no lit. lilac was, ach the sky's flank, colossus burgeoning mountains, I say, musing observing hurrying through hallways, beheading dandelions and rosettes, 'to my beloved lit. spirit,'

> my arms and hands regrind the floor, when I walk,

birds that, knock, at the window with their beaks, my empathy you know for pink balloons of hortensia, into the deep valley, namely, our glimpses that hand-in-hand out of the hillsides,

> 21.9.18, when I awoke the sky was overcast and a few bees,

he was as if swept away, for a number of weeks now I haven't heard or seen a thing of him whereas *bone-deep* in desolation I what had happened ...... I don't know any more what friend Christof looks like when I was lying in hospital for a long time I didn't know what my flat looked like any more when summer was over I searched the skies for the swallows that had *gone back home* when I awoke the sky was overcast, with bee and breeze at the window dear me! over and over the word RHUBARB escapes me but the stork feet of the rhubarb were red. Back then when I laid my hand in the bocca della verità although I was afraid of it being bitten off, I remembered the way the wisteria hung down deep,

> you're blue wisteria heath-dog violet you're a lit. frame you're a robin in the open air you hang off balconies Bad Ischl Hotel gold. Ship, namely, tons of parents, over and over I dream of walking,

back then they were standing by the open corridor window of the hospital with the new-born in their arms and Mama kissed the tiny hand and smiled, on the kitchen table a gentian blue something ...... in the photo Sophie, 3, with a boy's cut at the swimming pool,

> losing myself in his woods puzzling over Max Ernst's *Forest and Dove*, found a half-show I'd really like go into the woods, etc., FUCK ART / a bushel of tears, on the kitchen table, namely, a Meissen bulldog! my time is past my eye stuck to morning : something

suddenly gets stuck in my head suddenly something has surfaced that never was there before, deep dark morning it's rained, on the sheet a pink impression of your mouth, my lit. Adonis rose, etc.,

how the white spots stagger out of the sky! who's that knocking? as if someone were knocking at the window who woke me up maybe a bird knocked at the window and me out of sleep, I'd taken her to heart but for the last few hours now, *she was unparalleled*, perhaps a corona or the beginning of a new season (winter, for example), in the pink evening sky a LUCIFER,

3.10.18, she's got Type-2 diabetes,

the admonition : the blushed cheek's epiphany …… in the
waiting room : standing at the doctor's waiting-room window,
I said, namely, observing the yew which had pressed itself into
the garden courtyard, I said, a conversion, namely, the poet's
epiphany : the summer's whereas the proverbial silence of the
colourful ornamental fish in the aquarium, I mean, inaudible
orchestra, etc., in the back-most corner of the waiting room,
that is, establishing a trade name for a glowing summer's day
when we sat at a cafe : or in the garden courtyard of a building
in which a half-naked woman beneath coltsfoot leaves!, I said,
was sitting, the green painting reminding me of MONET, a
kind of mirror-like apparition, I said, whereas the half-naked
woman was reflected in the painting, I said,

> rather leaning on the waiting-room window and
> admiring a yew pressed against the wall of the inner
> courtyard, a boring aquarium in the back-most corner
> of the waiting room in which the colourful ornamental
> fish were still, observing, I dreamt of billions. Of lit.
> fish in the depths of the Adriatic with their half-open
> mouths sucking at divers' limbs, I said, *such goodies of*
> *toes*, isn't that so,

had he lost face, namely, weight?, he looked like a delicate boy,
with grey hair, I said, a late-summer morning like a corncob,
you know, something had shifted a bit the panties had shifted
a bit, she said, on just such a day one cannot be carried to the
grave : a day like a corncob with a banana-shaped moon, I say,
avant-garde, I say, ripped tulip, I say, dishevelled night, in a

photograph the poet with a WILTED bouquet he'd been given
after the reading, etc.,

I was asked if I'd known, Heiner Müller, yes I said, in
the U-Bahn (one day) once I helped him into his coat
to pay homage, to him however he cried '*I will never
forget this*!'

5.10.18, rock solid, he
said, a kitchen-allegretto!,

homage to Antoni Tàpies, are you a court-painter you've got torn *teats*, I mean, when suddenly Robert H. was in my way, I caught a glimpse of him as a figure in a Fr. film ...... the other day I saw a yng. Alsatian CROUCHED beneath a chair outside and felt his presence as he was watching me, Antoni Tàpies : *Chairs*, *White Cross*, ruffles of woods, *2 Feet*, I mean, while we were sitting there, on the dainty balcony of Villa Wassermann, during a storm, you were wearing a black hat, balsamic, the flash of our eyes in the dining hall of Hotel Erzherzog Johann, the bleeding and blinking of the sun, flaxseed strewn into my *peepholes*, *Tending the Oxen*, *Headboard with Fabric*, *Painting with Headers*, Shitao : *2 Men on a Rock Sitting by a River*, 1695, the fir trees *downwards* = growing into the valley,

> well yeah, the potted palm has brown leaves : fans in brown = nights you snipped off their tips with your scissors, how often their spines stung my hands! who was talking about the *red-cheeked*! *red-haired fruit*, a chestnut in the left tennis shoe,

incessant these shadows from the birds' wings as they fly past ach how it unnerves me, ach my indolence, ach the Institute of Lit. Vipers, she says, where at best. Our love story began, etc., 'Wotan's Vertigo' (is a plaisir?)

> I mean, your foot your feet that I'd like to kiss them, *Carré rouge*, 1976, aquatint-etching, stamped, 63 X 90 cm, ach pilgrimage of sleep ach blackbird swept clean NY,

ach woodflowers, a ripped chestnut leaf ...... very carefully, I opened up my eyes in the a.m. and held them open, more or less, with chopsticks whereas a fairy-like form of wax with pointy breasts *snatched* a lit. box, etc., what's Antoni Tàpies holding

in his arms? a panther an album a rabbit an asymmetry a chain of hills? I remember you jumping up out of our bed one night and somewhat Arabic-like (with a bay leaf) turning off the dripping, water faucet, Cy Twombly *Delian Ode* = thicket of scribbles, female breast with nipples (crossed out),

> 11.10.18, in unsleep :
> you daub a strand of hair over
> the left ear, etc.

.... ✂ .... = a really sm. pair of scissors on a piece of paper, was unsure from which direction the tolling of bells to my ears, 'the Nought.ies' (Marcel Beyer),

> why are you such a sweetheart, to me? Presumably because I shall soon be dead, o.k., red flecked cup with a handle like painted nails, which me to shedding tears. We were sitting in the Hall of the Muses = ALBERTINA!, or back then on the Cobenzl and looking down onto town which in the sunshine's, I mean, silvery gleam, etc., Vienna's *strass*, whereas in the stairwell my friend came towards me and we kissed,

back then with Klaus R. in Venice : hopping over the puddles and you unveiled me = turned cartwheels over the bridges,

> I'd like to see Philipp again who's living in a group flat ...... when he was young plunging his hands, into the Donnerbrunnen fountain so that they'd be clean enough to greet me,

>> Feelings of yew, namely, lace-up shoe of stone, found in the Adriatic, crakow. Presumably she'd had, something to drink, you say, ach variations on SORROW ...... o, you, my Engadin! as if of snow your angel! this fresh snow = this winter discharge,

how one crossed out the inadequacy of a sentence, Mama hated card-playing, liverwort up the slope, I mean, above the meadow *going up the stairs*!

Antoni Tàpies *Scissors in a Circle, an Inclination of the Letter T*. This eternal fever, with crop, over winter grasses : hare with crop, flying, Sakai Hōitsu *Rabbit and Autumn Grasses*, green line of plant-script, etc., you're quite wrapped up : top secret. Bird of prey with left talon pressed on breast, bird of prey grabs rose with right talon,

'what was that painter's name whose funeral you attended even though you didn't know him,'

13.10.18, lit. spider broke
my heart!

dear me in my dreams always looking for you but you're always lost in my dreams dear me the nights so long but the days too short back then with Mama in the garden of D., flower-enbushed garden house, etc., a *window-lumpen*! Dear me how subversive this spring still-life with ivy = Matisse, model wearing a helmet, breasts like lit. apples ...... a lit. winter, you say, soon lit. winter but, the afternoons still warm let's sit with the wind. Pressed to the building wall, etc., then flew off : with the wind flew off in tears, namely, the withered bushes, I mean, I say to Stefan Fabi do you remember how the storms *rushed* past when last April, you came to visit me you were sitting at the window when the sun in your hair, rushed, your yellow hair a nest in which the sun, rushed,

last April we roared, with the storms the stormy firs. Their wings. Antoni Tàpies' *Materia Colʒe* : devastated arm with sweet bandages,

glass balls in which a BAMBI! Lit. night gown a broken bird's nest, on the nightstand an art card from Antoni Tàpies it's a secret, I say, a drop of blood on the blanket,

...... Lake Gosau's feathers as if anchored we are in one another, your lit. crimson tongue, on the kitchen floor, a parable on the kitchen table : this word was lying on the kitchen table, with ink black tint / tusche on the blanket, in the a.m., the white clouds of

the blanket and traces of red : 2 red birds, that is, traces
of red birds red felt or blood, etc.,

'what necromancers the nights are!', I say,
budding Giotto trees, now, I'm exhausted,

19.10.18

into the eye, I say, into the blue eye, my tiny hand clutching the grandmother's hand …… she had picked me up and put me onto a bench in Rubens Park winter '27 I didn't yet know about Rubens' *Lit. Fur* (though, Grandmother's fur cuffs!) winter's white pearls / blossoms back then no one had drilled through my earlobes, I would wear a white fur hat, I say, did I have a bit, a bit of a squint?, you say, all lit. kids squint a lit., you say, the following night as a pearl / godparent / godchild, indeed I didn't know a pearl hung in the sky, didn't yet know the white birch trees in the park, winter '27, *who took our photograph?*

> it tasted / good to me, last night a lukewarm potato with skin, a lot, the tears, namely, the tears the pearl necklace of tears,

> 19.10.18, winter's
> adornment ('27)

the 4 stages of life (in the midst of bird nature) : after Stefan Fabi :

Lorenzo Lotto? in the a.m. I saw a few watercolours of clouds in the window which I, wanted to touch : they were a light-blue scream, etc., they moved from west to east, I mean, a lit. cloud like back when because so brittle they hoisted you over the snowdrifts (should one call it something like 'dish of winter-nature'?, ach on the sheet a lit. pink mouth ......)

> Klima's excitement, you say, I clung to myself like Charlie Chaplin on the hour hand of the cube clock, in order to stop time as she breathed away this time-whore, etc., how time fidgeted : over a snowy Alp : nightmare, namely, around midnight : nightmare as I had my right ear you know, *hello!*,

I ploughed the snow, nights, listening to *the voice of the Lord*, to your voice from next door, seeing eyes everywhere! dogs' eyes, fisheyes, on the parquet, your lit. red tongue = TONGUELING = fallen onto the kitchen floor,

> .... ach
> decades of aquatint

> in the colours of green and blue and yellow and red, and black, ach the colour of child-hood was red, the colours of adolescence green and blue, whereas the ochre-coloured shadows of the migratory birds (which at summer's end, fly to the south),

have you done something out of spite?

at long last into the black! maybe a corona!
namely, the beginning of a new season some-
thing like winter like death!

such a tic! *in the lift's mirror*! as we were cowering in the lift with
warped, I mean, expressions! of the artificial ROMAN! that all
eyes swimming in tears,

the blue blouse's neckline, I mean,

1.11.18, *gracious* cafe
where back then you,
stopped by, reading
in a book, fringed
lit. woods, farewell,

the engaged / no longer spot of colour (like Kafka!), dear Sra. Birgit : thank you for the ASSISI-card, I mean, thinking of me, we too think of you often, 100 years ago was in Mariazell, devotional objects richly illustrated, bought. You once said to me, we are already at the top of the mountain bound to each other even if we, a moonlit night. As I am very old, I have become very slow I see a golden harp in the window vis-à-vis, I prefer to write stenography : save a lot of time that way, soon we are going to bring you a Mozart torte with a lit candle

puff, on my leg or taste of my senses!

> he had a kind of sports cut = sports cap, I smiled magically, magical SAVINGS, first as a cashier, later he offered SAUSAGES, etc., but one day he disappeared : a halo how he spilt café au lait,

a dot = dear uncle! = deep-blue : I devilled off with Pessoa = Papa, into Café Schlusche (on Wiedner Hauptstrasze),

I write PROEMS

'I am neither in a good mood nor fed up' = Guilhem de Poitiers, green as moss, you say, the woods' sparks, etc., you *daub* strands of hair over the left eye!, parable on the kitchen table this word was lying on the kitchen table, this word fell out of my mouth, TURNER too in the a.m. (Papa with toothpick instead of cigarillo between his lips, you say, the evenings lonely, you say, my heart in the zipper pouch, *something blew and blew*) ...... (at night I wonder whether I'll live to see the following morning),

4.11.18, my trap
my essayism this
black bird how it
BANGS against the
window,

well yeah, I fringed my skull against a, piece of furniture, I mean, *overkill*!

> it is 9. November 2018 around 30 years after the day when Mama stood at the open corridor window at Vienna Neustädter Hospital and caressed Ursula B.'s infant she held in her arms. Who, today = Ursula B.'s spitting image! = said hello to me, namely, when my future GP said hello to me, etc., so that I shed those tears I had back then when seeing the infant now, 30 years later, once again, *an enigma*, I say, Mama, namely, buried long ago,

in the WOOD-ARCHIVE, I say, either way, it came to pass from time to time a word that I'd been looking for doesn't come to mind but its equivalent = something like 'the hanging',

> have fallen into a state of tender neglect, I say, was astonished that your purple irises, I mean, the purple structure of your fingernails had adjusted itself to match the structure of your toenails, symmetrical and *Tirolian*, Hölderlin says 'the song may hardly disclose it' by which he, meant, birdsong in the burgeoning year, etc.,

the ears or my Engadin, O you, my Engadin as if of snow, the nylons or my Engadin, Stendhal wept when writing, when writing wept, you say,

I'd like to extinguish my destiny!

9.11.18

the ringing leaves to cover the apples, on the postcard you sent me (red-and-green-glass garden globes of roses in the cleared flowerbeds now, the leaves to change the colour of the apples ......), I dreamt, a brownish clothed wanderer lying in the brownish leaves, namely, *in the eastern half* of the dream, but in the sensations of the waking state how did we avoid, staring at the wanderer for so long, whereas Raoul Hausmann with whom I had a long correspondence. Said 'hello Miss M., traces of snow, I mean, in a photograph that, shows, me as a 3-year-old child, I found traces of snow in the tender eyes of the 3-year-old child of the female doctor in whose office I found myself yesterday evening. *Mirrored*.' This mastery of a child, namely ...... go on and look, you said, yesterday evening, the tender : pale : eyes of the child : an as-yet-unknown terrain of his life, I mean, thistle of dream, etc., 'a boy's cut', you said 'a boy's cut', caressing the hare's fur!

> stepping into the pub's garden, you said 'how small the garden's become', stepping into the pub's garden *at night*, you said 'how small it's become, and how the moon, shone!', stepping into the reading room, you said, 'how small the room's become, how small the lace-up shoe, you said, *at long last the High Alps running riot*!'

the clouds enthused as if he were leaning against the window and observing the landscape, we wandered into a wood into a piece of Waldmüller's woods, feeling of yew-apple roar *that an umbrella blew*, by God, the lampshade's bag, from the window saw *the fire* of the Church of Our Lady of Victory,

14.11.18, written
while listening to German
Baroque songs

there the birds flash Goethe's brothers , now and again a stormy
sky = August, the raven covered in flakes walked with a cane,
etc., secret letters to K., she asked *BLEU III* by Joan Miró, did
you receive my postcard, a long time now already Father and
Mother no more, in Bregenz last weekend thought a lot about
Father and Mother ...... such lampions, corona, I said, he liked
me saying corona that I *smuggled* corona into our conversation
that I made corona a subject of discussion,

> a feverish life! a beatified life! I cannot write a thing
> on Emma Kunz! Dear Hans Ulrich sadly I cannot
> write a thing on Emma Kunz : her life and work don't
> speak to me, the tears ROLLED down indeed, into
> the lily bush! I mean, the *fork-buffet* : an expression
> that's fallen out of use, etc., the fork-buffet's flame
> ignited in my THROAT!, this week for the 3. time to
> Café Sperl, she took photographs of me, as I was
> leaning against the wall, the sun the sunshine built a
> nest in his curls, she jumped through the hoops, like
> zoo or circus,

the female doctor jeered a bit, I mean, jeered a bit : laughed a
bit about the naivete of a face : in a photo, showing, an elderly
woman's face, strange that (I had to think) often about this fir
tree ...... didn't like that she said fir tree instead of Christmas
tree : this one was wearing silver tears instead of silver orna-
ments. It seemed to me that the Christmas tree was already one
year, namely, since last Christmas, *that is, in the war?*

a tiny bit of lovely snow (or scissors) had been drawn
on lit. bag I loved that tiny pair of scissors : it was to
roar and ring where, half-asleep, one, etc.

the blue and white CLUMPS on your blanket,

26.11.18, lit. calendar
namely, lit. red tongue
tongueling the whole
evening, listened to
Henry Purcell, with tiny
scissors the moon *ach the*
jagged, *moon*,

sodomy you say when this roe we *idolatrous*!,

> my lit. online-river = lit. foot today our first
> snow-rain snow-rose, etc., a few days ago the
> last cranes flying southward : hundreds :
> thousands in the blue

sky in double-wedge formation ...... the *FAZ* newspaper is
waiting for you! endless the physiotherapist's given name
seemed to me : VERA ...... with her hands she showed me
how fat she'd grown when an au-pair, the Kurtags devoted to
the piano 4-handed at the piano in the first lilacs : plumage of
the first lilacs, half-asleep, you say, bellflowers and thistle!, a
tiny lovely snow, that one should cut open the lit. bag there!,
clump of a half-moon = waning, Cretan jenny,

> my glance out the window 6 o'clock in the
> morning, it is 28 November, waning moon :
> MAGRITTE, first snow thin first snow, she
> laid her lng. braid onto my blanket, glissando,
> 'sheathed-hands', in

the bar on the corner they play *darts* I'm afraid to go inside,
because of my eyes!, you know, do we want to cut the potted
palm's fans?, dear me my undulating lit. river lit. foot, the white
keys of a piano of snow on the roofs, when I moved I had to
leave my old concert piano from 1889 in the old flat I'd grown
so fond of, she left her lng. braid behind on my sheets, dear me
this lit. basket of sun how it totters this tiny lit. mug

ach why these diminutives all the time?

well, yeah, your charming kitchen, you say, the piece of music
on the GRAMMO went silent, the composition of a grass, in
1971 we travelled from Cologne to Berlin that the Rhine, that
the glorious Rhine greeted us with its spirit-kisses and -bites,
'pug with studded collar' with a black face, Meissen pug of
porcelain, back then we were sitting on the steps of the gallery
'next to St Stephan' and *drew you rather bird*, on a lit. piece of
paper, I said to you do we want to fly to Nice, a lot of things
have become lost to me, I say, even the books I wrote myself,
autumnal storm too, *rushed*!, hardly know the titles of the books
I wrote myself, ach dried flowers in your letters to me, or you
drew lit. stanzas in stenography which close to my heart,

                              28.11.18, the stormy
                              firs, the nerves,
                              namely, notice that,

found in my *pocket* : I cried : 'to the black camel' : beletage 2, you're my heavenly father = *Palermo*, more or less, performance. I dreamt! : a *hedge* = which brushed my shoulder, behind a park fence, namely ...... had I not complained all the time about this and that, in other words, what all escaped me, isn't that so, ach the most adorable, recommendations, passed me by, tiny glass with a handle = lit. mug, painted in the lovely colours of the Clock Tower in Graz, dear me beautiful birds fluttering, in the aether, etc., the lovely purple bush and branches, were withered, rustled / roared / in the vase (emancipated polecat on the cover of an animal magazine, *I mean*, *DELIGHTFUL* what a childhood word,

> my mother this bleeding foot painter), someone was
> said to have, pushed her, off the top of the mountain,

she had an expansive port-wine stain : blood-red hands, upon my forehead an image of Africa!, I mean, a *stork-bite*, upon my forehead a port-wine stain, yew roar, enormous half-open cloud-eye *of blue* in the east, the lovely purple bushes = ruffles were wilted = wasted, always inner courtyard, yew, spreading its arms, leaning against the doctor's waiting-room window, whereas the birds in the branches, *I mean*, *Minerva*, conclusio, namely, reseda plants,

> that you always wore a *head covering*, namely, *asser-*
> *tion*, during the war, at night we went walking that the
> backlit advertisements along the flaps of our coats,
> prevented running into other pedestrians, those nights

of bombs, you dragged your left foot after you as if
imitating an injury, broken foot, etc.

early the northern range in the window understand me prop-
erly : the enormous pink clouds in the east from minute to
minute changing form and colour ach the drift of winter birds,

4.12.18, that a lit.
umbrella *blew* you a
miracle (farmstead
of feelings : cut-up
method ......)

early the northern range in the window, that was super!, you say now and again you dragged yourself : shredding one foot after the other, during the war at night went walking WITH BUBI, with backlit advertisements along the flaps of our coats : to avoid running into other pedestrians, ach mountain of paper mountain of verse whereas a few flakes, clutched themselves, to the window, you know, that I incorporated the flakes ...... that was my wild puberty : I say : that when going out on hikes with my parents I walked fifteen steps ahead,

> someone did something bad to me or betrayed me, when we in the woods or by the lake, or had *washed away* my memory!, the lit. dress, namely, the child : of the child, THE FATHER WAS A RACING-CAR DRIVER! Mama even spurred him on!, wanted even greater speeds! : *flew!* through the lane of wild apple trees, the alternating appearance of language : disappearance of language : how do you explain that to yourself? it was in the '70s when we sat out on the lit. balcony *affixed* to the Wassermann house, ach jaunty shadow, Hans Hollein's shadow, a few years later we were sitting by a lake, or on a lit. white balcony whereas the woman of the house spoke of wanting to go to the kitchen to prepare dinner,

a real lit. gentian on the kitchen floor or the blue of lupines or I rolled around on the kitchen floor or carved a verse into white marble ...... a lot of things I can only write as I misread / mishear, *at the top* : I mean, *at the top* of the Dorfstrasze (have

I chosen the right word, here?) a book page opened : the powerful wheatfields ......

> 6.12.18, taxi, wood-kisses,
> ½ 5, sackcloth *uneven*, as
> he sat beneath the yew, from out of his coat
> pocket, 3 summers in a row missed the chance
> to adore the scent of jasmine (in City Park),
> whereas a lit. flag, floozy, lilac bush ...... in
> the early evening in lit., lilac bush ...... in the
> early evening DOZED OFF in the recliner,
> fell over de novo! awoke while falling, etc.,
> tree bark—what? what's wrong? bird with a
> white dress in the territory! spurred lan-
> guage!, told the Polish chauffeur, the story of
> my life, 'were you ever a singer, were you a
> diva', nights with Klaus Reichert at Café
> Central, I mean, your enchanted pair of eyes,
> 3 bottles of water *in tears*, *behind the blinds*,
> more or less I can only write something down
> as I misread / mishear, *that we howl* : *howl*
> *together*,

I really do require a muff *for my ragged*, feet, asleep I saw that
you were reaching for a pomegranate, robin of the highest
delight, tree bark—what! what's wrong? The rushing of the
winter bird ach peering wintertime, was it a mirage or *farm-
stead, of feelings*, archipelago of clouds,

in the a.m.? Apulia = watercolour with candelabrum (Linda
Waber), had someone ripped my clothes / ripped the roses off
me? a certain zenith in the street (the last words of May, etc.),
Heimito v. Doderer wrote me letters in various coloured inks
...... I liked to frequent the 'Nordstern' = cafe in Graz,

>I can recognize Pier Paolo Pasolini in a photograph by
>his flying arms (to keep his balance) while playing
>football but the photograph reminds me of *my aveng-
>ing angel*, I mean, exercises at the ice-rink when I was
>a child I think as a child with arms outstretched to keep
>my balance LIKE A STAND! : he, Pier Paolo Pasolini
>was like a bird with outstretched wings, but disap-
>pointed me because he worshipped football : a sport I
>loathe,

now when snow begins *to fall* I often think, I want to drive to
Falkenkrug brewery and there by moonshine, etc., am now
CHER LIT. CRIPPLE, that's according to Gertrud Kolmar,
in my daydreams ach I rediscover myself as a coloured photo
in my daydreams, I once ran into you in the woods, you, Adagio
in branches, another time we ran into each other at the airport
of Stockholm which took my breath away, (O.B.),

a bit sooty the window cushion, how so.

Archipelago of clouds (in the window), when I opened my eyes, from the window the fire of cherries, you say, the last words of May, a grate : gust : slide-in : the photograph of a shy Valie Export on some stairs, as Valie Export was leaning against the lift door, she tied herself together as if tying a package,

> 8.12.18, like
> falling stars the words
> came to mind, etc.

ach what an arcadia in the sky (in the a.m.!) Zuckerkandl in the sky too, I hear Swedish in the sky think I can understand a lit. a few numbers : the one and the two and the hundred : delightful diversity / cannot do math in my head, yes we laugh a lot, I've got whooping cough, witch's hair, Miramare, Telefunken, you write me 'what kind of avant-garde theatre was on Hamburgerstrasze?', when he was 4 years old Günter wanted to go pick flowers with his mother, meadow overflowing with violets but she could not grant him that *purple wish*,

P.S.: nettle locations?

circa woodshade and liverwort deep in the garden, more or less the buds : the calls, of the long-tailed mountain cuckoo, embracing the sparrow-wall, etc., it was by the lilac bush I said to Stefan Fabi, last time you were sitting in the sun (by the window) and the sun in your blonde hair, I mean, in the b/w photo ......

> I was around 3 : when Uncle Adi took *me up into the Rax*, carrying me on his back, whereas the rack railway, I mean, *and ate off painted plates*, it was 1929 that

my parents rushed to Nice in their car, and Papa whispered 'make sure that I don't get sunburnt', etc., but Mama had dozed off, highborn angels' tongues of sun,

> 'the word PROLES from your mouth', I say, how unusual, she reached for the pomegranate in the box, dear me, I've got sneakers on the sand

Found in Cattolica, they were tied together, back then, did I ride papier-mâché elephants, what an opportunity / how embarrassing when Mama would daub : tap me on the tip of my nose, such *lit. bird clothes* in the homestead, you call, today's a blood moon!, today I dreamt that I could walk again,

> wandering through some woods : a piece of Waldmüller's woods, 11.12.18, shall we go out : extinguish, like candles?

so many cheeks of post, the uncle carried me on his back, up
into the Rax, what a *bewitched* of snow, 'this pin-cushion', so
Marcel B., piccole tazze, so Marcel B., tiny cups, had he indeed
forgotten, *to close*, the parenthesis, or intentionally left the
parenthesis out from the end of his text? dear me your
wood-kisses, winter's iron curtain, it was CLEAR AS THE
SUN to him. As he said so, I was surprised at his use of such
an expression,

> I mean, *the lit. parquet*! : whenever we came by the lit.
> parquet you said, 'what a shame! a cafe would've been
> more appropriate here', the lit. parquet was well lit,
> and the like, I mean, the lit. parquet would also have
> been suitable as an aviary, while I was *lingering around*
> at his a black bird flew into the west window, oh lit.
> sister how your tears sparkled!, this past green summer
> in the crosshairs, an artichoke = dry-point etching by
> Louise Bourgeois, *Topiary* 2005,

with lit. robin, into the open air, then a half-naked woman
walked into the garden in the grass as if from Monet, I mean,
lit. coltsfoot woods, I dream of walking,

namely, tons of parents

a winter's Inverness cape I write proems, more or less
BLOODMOON : 25.1.57, it was 1929 that my parents rushed
to Nice in their car *and Papa said* 'make sure that I don't get
sunburnt' but Mama had fallen asleep, ask A. K., are you

driving to the Croatian, or what : Croation lake? *have idolized lit. parquet* I idolized the lit. parquet, OK!

18.12.18, that a
puddle of tea, namely,
lit. parquet,

Tàpies' crosses, almost full moon already : *shreds of leu* I was
grown today is 26.12.18, the swarming blooms, the corn poppy,
I collide into Van Hove : from my heart : on the street corner,
more or less. In the middle of grasses, I mean, whenever I write
letters I'd like to write stenographic abbreviations, how streams
flow out of our eyes, we celestialized ach we celestialized meta-
morphosized in a wood, in a piece of Waldmüller's woods I
heard the playing children, I fell in love with tiny scissors min-
imal scissors, roar of clematis, you know, an apple's cheek (so
green!), on the way here, so Bodo Hell, *a deacon with a perm*!,
pear : planted myself!, I ask you 'does the word PAIN-OPERA
exist?', the general din ......

> an epiphany, I say, an epiphany of the blushed cheek,
> a day like a corncob, pale daytime moon ...... later
> the snow melted I learnt to understand the language
> dear language blood moon on 25.1.57, I write / I
> scream proems, a tiny snow : tiny scissors, *what what?*
> past 9 o'clock : thought ¾ 2, winter's iron curtain, lit.
> wreath of freshly fallen snow, on the greeting card
> *Daisy*! as if it were another for snow *or what? or what?*,
> the lit. scissors ✂ I think of you things have grown
> dear to my heart, all of this, drove past the building
> where once I'd lived, with tears, I mean, from a window,
> Mother waved after me (as I hurried down the lane),

back then so many snow-white years ago!, a miracle, in the a.m.
as I, flipped open, my eyes, etc., half asleep : I'm said to have a

touch of Slovenian from Grandfather's side, fell : foundered onto the LIT. PARQUET, you know, foundered : fell into the open grave, swantje! swantje! are you a swan? a black swan? I dream of walking,

how Mama stared!

26.12.18, your pout,
you say, formerly atremble,
dear me I cannot find
my friends' phone
numbers any more ......
I have *learnt a few by heart*,
etc.

were in the realm of shadows? this wallpaper fairness! Wood etchings on wallpaper, from the '70s, I've sent you a photograph of the work *Form-Pair* which consists of 3 parts, combined into a tower, are we standing in front of wallpaper, I mean, the sky's wallpaper, lit. sky like wallpaper, played with blocks, as a child, etc., on the piano = played a roaring glissando of airs, it was by the lilac hedge, I say, last time you were sitting in the sun (by the window) and the sun in your blonde, hair, I mean, in the b/w photograph, I think about you things, have grown dear to my heart,

> dear me, we were standing in front of the wallpaper *Form-Pair I*, 39 x 45 cm, wood etching on wallpaper, was I next to you, was I behind you had a pale serious face, lit. letter, you say, lit. letter (tons of parents), I'd have loved to lead you through the castle garden, SO I accompanied you in thought, Bolzano!,

were we 2 merging forms? if it rained if flakes were laced like back then on Museum Island (Berlin) perhaps we'd nodded off?, *the betrothed colours*!

> did he ever give me a flying cap as a gift? : 'but she's really got to wear it too!'

highborn angel's tongue of harmony ......

30.12.18

'the Christmas tree like fretsaw-woods, tic or Tieck as we went down in the lift, hovering, "making faces" in the mirror, as if a tic, was it, a tic that we flattered, each other, buried in one another, in the lift mirror, downwards, Tieck or tic, 'yng. people alone, and *piercing*!, already 3 January, I liked that photo with Arthur Miller, a bloody aria, namely,'

> Send me, a few of your lines so that I can add some drawings to them, so Stefan Fabi, pumped the old draw-well empty back then in D., I had such a brooch, winter brooch!, so fine with a bird's beak : open wide as thirsty (in the past I always wanted to drive to Andalusia when I hear the word Andalusia now, I have to cry, Christa Kühnhold often walked around her *tousled* garden, but now it doesn't belong to any one), dear me.

On that day we fidgeted across the rotten balcony with its view onto deep-blue Mondsee lake, I was afraid of collapsing, namely, into the profoundly deep. Lake, etc., as a child I learnt : horizons *blowing all-too-blue*, this and that calamity would have careened into me,

> whereas the wood-kisses, the setting sun, reflected in the water, I mean, you simply lay your clothes under the bushes before stepping into the floods ...... before you ascended descended the rungs into the lake, on the

veranda the full bowls of fruit, the wasps' full waistlines, ach the development of the new world has become incomprehensible to us, will become ever more incomprehensible, you say, high time to

MAN THIS DOLPHIN!

leave, (as if the Grammo gradually went silent, what counts are the incomplete sentences, blue impromptu blooms, my sleeping feet : with heavy heart, tiny lovely snow, archipelago of clouds in the a.m.), I've got to wait a while = a few hours and days before continuing with the writing so that I don't repeat myself,

just in the lit. skull, all administered, I watch myself, etc.,

5.1.19

what is NATURE prompting us? what is ART prompting us? more than everything, the woods kiss us ach how the woods kiss us, lit. wood, kiss! the cherry-pairs sing, creaking lettuce, how the morning light like the talons of morning, cheek cut or itching, I mean, Stefan Fabi's love and glory, suddenly appeared in the hotel lobby, that I, stretched out, my arms, to express the joy of reunion, more or less a furioso, for heaven's sake water-colour on cardboard, embedded in landscape : 7 women = Pleiades, 210 x 105 cm, wood etching on canvas 4–14, cheeked pink-cheeked : Woman Number 4, never before did any thing similar appear (to me), pink-cheeked sucking my lips, etc., kneeling cloverleaf instead of heart, feathers instead of hair,

> behind the yew hedge : Pleiades, the light-blue watercolour of the Croatian lake, the sky's light-blue BLOOM, cut wallpaper with really lit. ✂ ('scissors'), tiny lovely snow, what counts are the incomplete sentences!

ach! diffused in the tram!

I've fallen in love with NATURE I've fallen in love with ART, figure of a 'self-portrait' (figure of wood placed against the wall, the viewer can look through the 2 holes in the box and take up the figure's perspective : original size *c.* 1.70 m tall, etc.), as well as me, pressing myself against the entrance door, through which the view enlarging optic of the peephole peeking / peeping, a colossal slogan = l'art brut, knicked papillon

...... namely, out of wood, what did I spy through the PEEP-HOLE? what the figure through the peepholes of the box? something like glimpse into lit. wood, onto a lit. river, onto poetry's steps, etc., or like back then in City Park the view onto otherworldy wilds, isn't that so,

> I mean, Stefan Fabi's bread with honey, a
> *blizzard*, namely,

> > 11.1.19, sent me letters
> > in which wilted
> > flowers, I mean,

after reading a few of Heiner Müller's poems, you send *me*, a few sentences too. You send *me* a few luminescent sentences too that'll inspire me to paint something, etc., whereas my right eye sewn shut comes from my dreams, my right eye like the moon is, daytime moon, *Ganymede*, the speaking of language, place of screams, animals' bray : gentle animals you all consume, place of screams, listen!, for days this scream of mine expelled in my ears. As I was falling down,

> when a dog on the other side of the street looks at me I am myself the dog that's looking at me, see, I am the dog that's looking at me, *grass-green in spring*, my diet : pull grass, they say. There will be rain, as a dog I hound (you hound) through the meadows you cannot think cannot speak but the honeymoon, I mean, I bark at the honeymoon am I a gentle animal which out of your hand. Eats, Was I a fish or lion, or a silver penguin in the Antarctic, how I thrilled!, I and also shed tears silver tears, the flying automobile, and roaring the sun ...... chaos' *clou*, went on a leash, I mean, passing water,

I mean, revelled in the garden (in Bludenz in your blood), *nosing the path* what a lit. dog, I am, love and glory, JD speaks of nervousness on its knees, something like a Spaniel. *That we this roe idolatrous,*

> my glance out the window 6 o'clock in the morning today is 13 January 2019, waning half-moon : *Magritte*, into the beloved bush (as if I had whiskers),

13.1.19, the title of this
poem could also
be 'to my ascent',
will someone cook something
for you? ach the *rustic*
woods ......

that's psychological you say, namely, the meadow or
passing water. That we this roe, *idolatrous*, I've fallen
in love with tiny ✂ (scissors), etc., leu, etc., learnt
about the legend of the big bang, sitting on an abstract
DIVAN (with female hare in what's left of the snow,
namely, profile), on noble branches of the universe
your nightly drawings of light which you with white
chalk, I mean, white pocket torch-script the starry sky,
you revealed to me, that is, sweetest star-threads, etc.,
how ravishing the choreography of the heavenly bod-
ies, *of the moon as well*! its appearing and disappearing!,
our formal skin, I mean, the beauty of emptiness, the
idea : vessel : from the thirst that tortures us (or
what?), the vessel of my hands when a child, to suck
the fountain, that is this perpetual BUBBLING of the
yng. Danube : in Donaueschingen, as over my wrist,
this bubbling which my inflorescence, nutshell, lakes
and seas ...... dear me : written if unsaid, sitting on
the side of St Cecilia which the language of the organ,
namely, the buds that live within me, I recognize : *so
grumbling* the universe, ach so slow the pulse of the
all, I mean, *halo of matter*, etc., Mother's dominant
green, skyward, that is, the kiss-landscape, wormholes
in the lit. clouds / the golden section, any thing can
be a model, ach hearing and smelling a Beethoven
sonata robs me of my senses. The eyes of the dove, *for*

heaven's sake the heavenly bodies, we crinkle twilight's sash, bundle the horizon together, in tears : pin the moon,

 everything just not eternity. Dear me, ANNE, by Paul Valéry, LANDSCAPE, or rustic, woods

23.1.19

indeed you me snowdrop cheeks so white lit. animal, namely, in the lit. handled glass with white strings tied shut its white-green neck they drink a lit. *booʒe a lit. too* from the handled glass (at night) you hear them ringing, looking out the window calling spring (enough to make you cry you know to communion!) they smell what do they smell of, they smell of *deep* grass there where once we *deep* embraced white-green morning dew on your eye, they can speak too, I never would have thought!, a collage by Max Ernst, the wings of the flower petals ......

we, however, are going through hell, oblivion,

22.2.19

this is how I see it before me. In a photograph made of a head : my head seemed, a stem, to sprout (as a caress that might rise from the dead) as behind me from a vase that one cannot see : sprouting stems : the photograph seems rather patient my head seems pensive, my eye stiff ...... on the backside of the photograph stands '20 / 12 / 11' : the date of its appearance you say, a Dürer hare at the nape of the neck / garden branches, of.

> glorioles of blackbirds the apparent contact comrade
> blackbird at the window *picking* ...... on a foot on a
> snow white-green lit. mouth SPRING, etc.

23.2.19

the night's full moon and the night's blood moon it is although
a lit. bit sprouting (well yeah) a visionary with song, you are
my daily bread ...... once in deep memory, I see myself in the
open air *presumably a vineyard* read from my own writing,
bright yellow landscape, then he disappeared with his head and
wanted to kiss me but the lift opened in front of us and we had
to move apart,

> he was standing by a corner of the wardrobe
> and seemed to be thinking about something
> I knew that pose : his right elbow jutting into
> the air, and if anyone was close by they'd be
> speared it was a moment of concern, the
> dream of many a night that with my crutches
> into the terrain, I mean, the appearance and
> disappearance of sweet thoughts,

the shadows of the migratory birds = immortelles, at the end
of the summer, I write proems *I've got wood-inspiration*! broken
out my grandfather from the RUSTIC, woods, lit. uncle =
deep-blue I devilled off with Pessoa, ach bleeding country
house back then, 'Wotan's vertigo', shaggy world,

> 25.2.19, and you said,
> why are you such a *sweet-*
> *heart* to me, presumably because
> I shall soon be dead.
> And Peter Pabisch talked about
> prosody! or Sylvie

bemossed, we skyed with
our friends, there's an
unlucky star over Vienna, I
cried my eyes out,
etc.

a Trojan horse in the bushes or, winter's iron curtain

you're history : you're a bloodhound a bloody dog history, it occurred to me as a flash when waking up it roared off (damn : how it roared off) : I am in possession of the artist's sketch-book, namely, the grasshoppers of Lake Atter, the Book of Evening of the artist from Neumarkt 2002/2003 *in crimson*, you're a bad pear / theatre of stinging-nettle / you're a bad pear with a squinty eye! how off-putting : this horse's utters : off-putting just like the whole history ...... ach skeletonized horse : the tribulations of a Trojan horse! spring on the ottoman the wording like passing water, the concepts corridor and crape I experienced even the stones crying,

> 'I'd have loved to *pull* you through the castle park : on my hand', that's what you wrote me once—enough to make you cry to communion, hiatus and fantasy!,

The Trojan horse stepped into Yves Klein's blue wonder too, the brides of the wind too swarmed through the peepholes of the Trojan horse, remember the couple is in the egg cup, remember Mama KNOTTED a carpet with a Trojan horse!, hornets tonight, the history!, dreamt the word *vernissage*, in tears, and angry really angry!

> '*the Gelsen (gnats) of Gelsenkirchen I've gone insane*, you've got to crouch down and crouching have to fray the desolate brain, etc., am something of a Trojan horse myself, like that tangled mane, I'm a lit. cripple I am history,'

all the LEAVES of my conscience, back then in that open-air restaurant in Bad Ischl, thought of the word LEAVES : as with my back to the *trellis* : I mean, garden-loge, sitting, I mean, Tàpies' *armchair*, the rolled-up leg-warmers and sculptures, cross on the forehead, I'm drawing you a cross on your forehead ...... when you're overtired, really tired : eyes ready to close already, and nevertheless a word or half-sentence scratches becomes a *lit. animal* that crawls away, I feel really torn I've bitten my tongue, when I MISREAD something everything is saved when I MISHEAR everything is saved, found the artist's workbook again, it's rearing the legendary horse the sore battlefield-horse, ach the RUSTIC woods, I mean, crocus / cane had lost a cane in the woods, soul graffiti you are my daily bread ...... an admirer sent me a lit. bag of medicinal clay : I was supposed to swallow it but it horrified me, etc., I galloped over the hillside I was a Trojan horse,

'remember, on the lit. parquet : the troubles of history,
I mean, a Trojan horse's will-o-the-wisp',

3.4.19

to my honoured Doctor (NB),

a lit. pink cloud in the morning sky a bit like a lit. balled fist
my right foot how it glides to your examining hand : something
like due to veritable pump of blood. This life : a happening,
you say, Wotan's apron, in endless devotion, hope the writing
will pass off,

> on tippytoes, *the proem* must scamper, you know, and
> chirping!, ach the emulation of the beautiful, the rain's
> baptized children we, the new spring ...... golden rain
> of which you are native, etc.,

10.5.19

as I was blossoming (immense) so deeply. On behalf of Lake
Atter such blue tears as Prussian blue wound in the a.m., I
mean, mornings, I mean, cold, I mean, wave in the sky that I
save : *speak* accents of my language = currant-language, a
miniscule fame or praise, etc., the eye glued shut in the a.m. I
think it was in Casino and I had long legs,

> ach like cherries from your throat ach swarm
> of cherries, I think about you all the time and
> read your thoughts in endless devotion,

gnawed off lit. bone, basta!, ascot of Instagram, etc.

21.5.19

like, Velimir Khlebnikov, stone of the future

this animal keeper with a lemon-coloured bonnet and glasses :
sitting in front of her : yng. lit. brown animal in her hands,
namely, enough to make you cry with lit. red tongue (speaking)
like toy monkey in animal magazine = journal!, tonight such
hot, tears, I mean, shed. Like back then, in D., rain barrel in
the front yard inseminated with *bellflowers*

>   *'help me, sexton, I'm tired*!'

ach lit. primadonnas I will *thunder about* on the lake's back,

>   This morning when I, stepped, outside the door I saw
>   a number of trophies = rugs one on top of the other
>   hanging on the stairs next to them a big round cactus,
>   *'come my friend into our cottage you go on along first*
>   *—I'm going to linger about outside a lit. longer before I*
>   *follow ......'*

This morning when I, stepped, to the window Futurism's ban-
derole appeared to me the language of lambs too! sitting with
a common pipistrelle in an aviary : everything is yellow is
green is violin, in a yellow cloud of devotion, and *'everything
blues'*, Margret Kreidl writes 'yesterday we were at August
Wall's exhibition in Gugging, in other words, in the middle, I
thought of you : your pathos HUMMED within me : still
saying hello to you HUMMING! I mean, LULUHONEY!'

>   I'm a fir tree have wolfish blood like Mandelstam, in
>   the twinkling of an eye in a meadow,

>>   *'storms in the month of MEADOW'*

today I tore out my tongue it's lying on the lit. par-
quet! Antoni Tàpies' spirals, Papa sitting immense
with the rosettes or rotundas, so :

played footsie! ach the buildings rolled down the slope / some-
thing like philosophy with goats,

2.6.19, *my fright* :
I am, frightened,

close to the flak tower, already roared, my fever, close to the
flak tower this lit. bouquet, of fever, then had diabolical neu-
ralgia, then there were these kind of tins with AGOPTON =
agaves and water lilies, etc., then Dominik Steiger ...... I had
a toy but I didn't know its name it was a particular drug I bit
my tongue, back then in Bad Ischl it was a toy or sparrow, I
mean, a handful of sparrow in a bush in a garden in Bad Ischl
there where we sat that bush with the sparrows in reality *a pile
of tears*!, only after a few months / years, did we find the time
to answer letters,

> how would have things gone between us = Traudl
> Bayer : yng. 22! had our paths crossed back then, when
> she said we're passing water, in Arenberg Park (or
> what), in front of the door to my flat an envelope with
> pale pink peonies or stanzas of pale pink peonies, I
> mean, there is a drawing of Mimmo Paladino's upon
> which your foot. A puppy lying in front of you,
> caresses, whereas your mouth.

>> 8.6.19, my roaring in
>> the bush, made
>> immortal by the nighttime
>> storm, etc., today
>> worked without music,

'today the first swallows flew over the VISTULA.
For Bernadette Haller'

around 1 in the morning a storm around 1 in the morning I
went to the window I saw myself go to the window I was alone
but had this secret, namely, in the swan-sky of Krakow your
lips de novo as big as an idea of grey tin something like a lit.
hand : an amulet of love = of the sea's waves, you had such a
sleep or veil (fame or praise or mountain lake!, you dreamt
about Ronda, the rose-vendor of Crete),

> what wild tears when saying goodbye, a grey
> lit. hand of tin, etc.

> 8.6.19, 'puristic
> eco-sky ......'

For Bohumila Grögerová for the lit. sword!

the last time she wrote was in coloured pencil and capital letters
because her *eye-mass*, in other words, informatics : she translated
Death by Muses into Czech, I remember in tears her beautiful
art, etc., there was that colossal suspension bridge over the
Vltava, in the early a.m. the fishermen in their boats, with Ernst
Jandl Bohumila Grögerová Josef Hirsal to SLAVIA, (like the
lit. Jesus), 'there are many connecting threads to her universe!'

> something like electricity and Vltava, I work
> a lit. bit as a painter, I mean, the colour grey
> like ashes like dust like sparrows like rain like
> dusk and elegance,

ochre-coloured mounted on heart. She said can you explain the
world to me, how I wept that the tram swayed one time tilted
to the right another to the left,

> 3.7.19, 4.7.19, we
> called her 'Bohunka'
> it was a long time ago very blue
> the days, it was
> as if she were knocking at the
> door, 1 time at night as
> the moon la lune, in
> every corner a delicate
> animal or line,
> *namely, a modernism*

(I remember 1 time in summer an EXCREMENT in her district whereas the stars. Josef Hirsal translated Ernst Jandl we were friends yes, great friends, *farewell* ......), *this is a proem* : it would have been 100 today I asked it 'were you a strict judge?'

> 'as a young judge I was strict as an old judge docile :
> *docile-as-a-lamb when you go into the water docile-as-
> a-lamb*' ......

in heels when you go into the water docile-as-a-lamb in heels when you go into the water,

> I am a foundling : pull a handcart,

12.7.19

one morning *c.* 2 weeks after your departure a dragonfly came through the window with arms outstretched said hello and stayed a number of days, soul graffiti (after Antoni Tàpies), around June : this July should I attempt to try out Ascension Day. You say while through City Park we, look at the ducks the ducks' feathers how they shimmer, namely, the wolves back then in 'Lit. Café' as our feet at the radiator (to warm them), we played footsie, how wonderful such winter-love ......

> winter's buds : *my senility*! fell asleep in the kitchen chair fell out of the kitchen chair, Georg Kierdorf-Traut at the moment southward, on the kitchen floor a man in a turban, I'm taking over! this intimacy that with an artificial gripper you pick things up off the floor (lit. parquet),

the clou : *I killed myself*!

> 17.7.19, this lit. lamp
> has gone out *farewell*,

I miss you I lost you in the woods perhaps in the larches in the dead nettles perhaps in a meadow in the middle of.

these are a lion's feet or those of a nun, etc.

well yeah you *destroyed* me, since the 19. year of your departure one of your poems in Georgian translation lying before me, namely, with a starched collar, etc.,

> the whole night long I saw your lion's feet before me, we were the rain's baptized children (evergreen), eating something like the freshly fallen snow with snow shovels ...... you are my daily bread : before us a line by T. S. Eliot 'consumed by either fire or fire', through the woods of Bad Ischl shimmered gown such a white gown,

18.7.19

LAMENTO

looking and listening, I mean, peeping and listening more or less clothing daubs and drops of eyes, namely, rolled from the meadow rolled away from the meadow, the parents standing, on the meadow, clapping hands while in the stream the *delightful* fish, I mean, fish in the mirror hello!, you pointed at some trout called out *those right there*!, wanted to eat them : beautiful trout!, you said those right there!, peeping trout you could sense your death, etc., do you remember : roof birds with unlocked beaks and white breast

  this bird on the roof bird with white breast (tears in eye), unlocked beak it screamed I'm thirsty!

  help I'm thirsty : my thirst as big as a king no rain on earth, such longing for the earth,

at long last he said that I'm a shaman!

  19.7.19, the sun's
  display makes us blind,
  etc.,

l x a night, in every corner a delicate animal or line, philosophy with a goat, etc., the sun's display makes us blind, she was wearing a lit. white jacket but there was a storm, in spring you've always got to cry or *most of the time* : Mama *most of the time* would stand at the open window and cry, looking *OFF-STAGE* : out the open window and crying (real quiet!), etc., she travelled, crying, to the Grk. island of Hydra, pretty chic, she said,

> we were standing in the lift going down!, and I said mauve to you, you repeated the colour = mauve, we were sitting by the open window, watching the evening clouds and said at the same time MAUVE, Mama was allergic to the heat, we're going to the *Alps* around Trieste, one time we were walking through the woods, someone hopped over the lit. roots but I didn't know them maybe a relative of Matisse whose wall-paper,

you send me too, luminescent sentences which will inspire me to paint, or mountain flowers, whereas my eye is sewn-shut, once again we turned our glance back : the mountains were already cloaked, namely, by the beautiful evening, isn't that so, I put the word TABOO all over my workspace, which reminded me of the 1. Film I was allowed to see as a child and was called TABOO ...... the final sequence showed a drowning swimmer, *arms grasping for help*, upon his high forehead the words : I've got a wolfishly glowing heart, I've torn out, my tongue : it's lying on the *lit. parquet*,

31.7.19, ornithology,
or how thirsty we are!

from Vienna General, the
black flag waving,

the antipodes of the hare, you know, of the mountain's roses I remember how I shivered (the eyes *gummed up*, Christianly gummed up, come on we're going ice-skating with *senescent* quail and titmice a bit thin already the bushes). In late August, the country inflamed this summer, back then we hiked to the quarry Mother and I, with the watering can in D., dear me stopped with Father in front of the shop window for a long time so that he *could linger*, namely, like flowerbeds, etc., I mean, thinking of the JOYS of a late August there the shadows of the shadows of swallows (breaking to the south),

> the monstrous rushing of time, I mean, wasn't it just winter : and now the boldness of a new season, how it breathes in / out, etc., the swallows' adornment

> *are they a gay couple?*

back then in D., cart paths black with *crushed*, I mean, elder-berries, delicate clouds in the a.m. = clouds = Claudia Larcher's ROOMS

> *bilingual, namely, the trees,*

> > 4.8.19, so that he
> > *could catch his breath*,
> > veritable ...... ach I felt
> > like a
> > poppy flower, he'd place
> > a poppy flower in all

his letters, later I learnt.
I learnt that the crow
with which the poet
spoke was stuffed. Winter
perhaps or Elysium, an
adornment of moon,

like streams my streams of tears sprang, I was lizarding :
namely, choking as I *incorporated* my breakfast, I mean, sitting
at the breakfast table whereas a pair of IMMEDIATE flakes =
flora at the window, knocked, namely, like lit. birds, etc., I
mean, that your lit. pink tongue ach how it fell,

> so much has become lost to me, even the
> books I wrote myself, I mean, Brita S. con-
> jured up a few damp lit. roots or long steno-
> graphic lines ...... which to my heart, in
> other words, like gnawed-off lit. bones, etc.,

today the last swallows flew over the Vistula, you were hoping
for just such a sleep or veil, namely, a swan-sky, *the lit. ear*
(30.3), holding a word tight in the moment of awaking, tip, e.g.
sky, half-asleep, you say, the blue and black

CLUMPS

I mean : on the blanket, etc., how embarrassing (when I was
lit.) when Mama would *tap* me on the tip of my nose,

> 17.8.19, *I'm taking
> over!,*

he says to me you're a steep dog, a lit. bit of medicine on the kitchen floor, I've been immortalized by the night storm, etc., wood-kisses as a child already playing matador ...... I wore SALAMANDER SHOES the world was going down in the window vis-à-vis a lit. table with 3 books one atop the other, *vis-à-vis something red*!, like a sleeping cap, in the egg cup the seahorse's lit. hand this symbol for infinity,

it was *c.* winter, *my eye bit shut*!, poetic pragmatism : I was sitting on a wooden bench behind me the bird-bush and wings, I mean, the wings at my back a titmouse got lost in my room : closet : he began to laugh when I said closet, a sudden green all of a sudden a sudden green, lane of hornbeams, I was a lit. kid : namely, stress or bouquet of red carnations, pink NORTHERN RANGE in the window, I squinted a bit from my head, the woods sprouted, did St Afra have flaming arms or flaming wings?, I dreamt of you and the Fr. flag, my dream : the lit room strewn with shed hair, isn't that so, my dream : female modernist modiste Mama sliding on the floor-brush : on one foot or leg (as if she were ice-skating!),

Uncle Rudolf with black cherry-eyes,

18.8.19, from the gala,
a perception, after
Winckelmann, my
sister within me,

182

18.8.19, from the gala,
a perception, after
Winckelmann, my
sister within me,

so blue-grey this world it was a baby Jesus ...... it's snowing
it's snowing it's the twentieth of August, a prose-like rhythm
how perfect! you are my familiar, in the pine-tree forest, in the
window vis-à-vis : the lit. organ, it was these mountains and
pasture-drunk, depiction of a siskin

in my dreams I still am young, in my dreams
I am high, was named ISEL after the moun-
tain where I the light of the world. In my
dreams I am young in my dreams I am high I
am such a crucifix et cetera, it blossomed the
like : he blossomed my whole hut full,

I'm the escaped one! St Afra, *sewing*, after JD, back
then with Mama wandering along the RAILWAY
TRACKS, I've got such a vein, I've got an eagle,
light-blue eagle in Trieste, my love for enveloppe
(Fr.), I mean, *sealed* envelopes, who used to always
send me letters behind a lit. sealed mouth?

overnight they had inscribed lit. holes in your
face, I remember : Valérie B. with the lit. bird
in the tree in front of the window, whispering
in Fr., etc.,

20.8.19, did I cross
myself?

(was it *c.* one winter on
the chamoir of the
dreamt
writing paper?)

P.S. summer '17 : read a lot wrote continuously, 2 weeks
ago : you begin with the *butterfly-stroke*, and SUPER-
NATURAL cold, aurora,

possessed some equipment : he possessed some equipment, *to pick up*, a thousand lit. pieces of paper off the floor, joli joli you poached about in my writing, I mean, that his masculinity from heaven, fell, I refreshed myself with flowers, embowered myself with apples, Valérie Baumann speaks French with the lit. birds in the tree in front of the window,

> if it's overcrowded, if it's overflowing, with blossoms with buds,

I dreamt of you and the French flag, my sister within me, in the veins of the Alps, Mama pawns her fur to the Dorotheum, but she will never get it back out, knee-length fur, from the '30s, dear me the shadow of a bird plummets into the depths, bilingual the yng. tree, have Mandelstam's blood,

> 'consumed by either fire or fire through the woods something like a shimmering gown, white gown, etc.,' no rain upon the earth, he said at long last, that I was a shaman, once I wiped up his sick as so withdrawn, etc., all that's left of me is prostheses, as this body so dissonant, ach lit. sword!,

you say sit down at the machine and get writing I can see the lines in front of me before I write them down, joli joli reading once again through *GLAS* half the night through,

25.8.19

I've got a pearl button on my brassier, rather heartfelt has got 2 eyes but, mouthless (moonless night!), on the way home I saw that the scythes (= suns) in the tops of the trees were hanging in the evening that I the tears, that the tears poured down that they ach! tortured, I mean, I caught a glimpse of my friend's shadow, etc., yes, cuddling the tiny bush on its headrest ...... the following morning the silken stream in front of the window : Rohrmoss : evergreen, etc.,

> one's just so happy in the WALLPAPER, I saw her from behind as she had a curly head = cousin-like!, we were sitting within the WALLPAPER = fairytale-like, with rhubarb juice, later I'd, RUN across a mountain meadow, whereas at the tops of the bride or brood that is brooding stars, I mean, Dublin's poetics ......

in the left wistfulness the shadow of the garden : a plum shrub, up above, summer's score, you know, laundry hung out on the balcony, the memory of Dachstein = dusk, lying awake for hours at night, the scree ...... on the blanket impulse of ink (Max Ernst), sitting a sudden half-minute of vertigo,

> they say it's his birthday today he is a lit. sheep and it's his birthday, your hand caresses my foot, namely, I wish that you would take my foot in your hand, because my toes hurt, I mean, you take my foot into your hand and let it rest there,

28.8.19, calendarwards,
the lit. ear, namely,
bush of crepe paper,
JD.,

you were sitting, how the sackcloth whispered : *slid*! into the mighty grass from out of your coat pocket, how cold the morning, a biscuit on the kitchen floor,

> our loved ones' *relatives* are actually our relatives : that is *the actual*! they've got the same whiskers the same lit. ears,

I was sitting on the balcony and saw how the flaming. Moon, slid down : slid down the mountain, I wrote you that on a post-card, out loud, etc., in the last moments of morning-sleep, an audition 'Kopf and head', 'Kopf and head' and the like, but I was making my way through the woods, gushing over a tiny chalkboard with a lit. sponge, it was the fear of death!, Mama removed a wine glass which had sprung from the cupboard, etc., today is 4 September '19, place setting for a left-hander, by Antoni Tàpies, it happened that my friend Marcel took the bouquet which I had received on the occasion of ......

> that he took this storm bouquet from me : I will not forget, brooch of dusk, the morning went by so quickly, a photograph showing me in a beret : pale ear sticking out of thin hair,

the swallows thither!, nevertheless, with the ravens in the garden, no one will ever know, know everything about me, like Mother would say during her last days, I cannot confide all of these things even to you : I will take them to my grave, etc.,

> 4.9.19, lit. spoon on
> the kitchen floor, purple
> day.

as the summer : how did the summer, scamper past, I mean, as summer bent into autumn's edge, and we were sitting out on the wooden benches and looking into the valley, isn't that so, into the sepia-coloured, do you remember, and all of a sudden a bundle of blooms : purple blooms, a bushel of tears and deer, bundle of deer how the summer scampered past!, etc., astonished futurum, you in the photograph with a bouquet, speechless, father's constitution, we drove through the lanes, *childhood's variety*, pater noster!, ach how it kneeled, endlessly kneeled! : the lit. notebook! down!

> *winter's adornment, namely,*

> > at night : autumn rain through the open window, there, your soul breathes its last, wild bushes grew out of your skull, AS IF SNATCHED FROM THE AIR : I feel robin's hands : clinging, etc.,

> aesthetic of my unsuccessful life, dear me ......

> > 8.9.19, by the time my glance turned back the mountains were already cloaked,

along the shallow river in D. the father stood he stood at his side lit. hand in a bowl, I mean, 'nature-writing'= presumably a buzzword, I write PROEMS, I write digitally, fear thundering, in chains I lay in *flower-chains* how the tears flowed, along the naked river, the wild herbs, to crouch down, as a child, whereas the mulberry fruit of D. shed its ink-black blood, etc., chaff of weeds,

> were they lines was it the beginning of a line
> were they Franz Schubert's *Refrainlieder*,

she was a bit quirky, I mean, THE QUIRKY ONE, is that how you say it?, I often don't know which word, namely, whether snatched from the air : this woman, I mean, this stranger at the hairdresser's with her tears for me, etc., woke up at ½ 4 with pain in my chest *uneasy* with you to the airport, many years have *elapsed*, my love, I wonder if he still plays violin at the cafe, a delightful soul, when early this morning I lay down on my right ear : LIT. EAR! the word *lit. spirit* occurred to me, how could that be, transcribed something about old Motti!, a ton of ink stains on the blanket, Pulkau flooded with trees : a raging river ...... then once again *listless*, my brain-reading, like Leibniz says, namely, the open books rustled, you're agave : bloodily enraptured, I pack my right ear in my headrest, gruesomely the waves of the lake hurt : when the sun *rummaged* about within them my sensitive eye, I mean, I have to my heart's content. That I held my hand like a dear protective cap, before my eyes, a kind of roof-garden like Hans Hollein's compositions in the Albertina (this roof) in particular when

Heinz Schafroth tarries among various sea cliffs, while the violet flower-carpet MOISTENED his theatre-eyes, isn't that so, ach how Samuel Beckett, interpreted, my poems, in which

> *a rebus,*

was hidden,

> > like my daisy-consciousness that produced wilted leaves and flowers, while the wild geese screamed above Lake Biel, overcome by a raptus, was,

> > > 13.9.19, fly with
> > > train, the chirping
> > > moon, I sense the scent
> > > of Dürer's violet
> > > bouquet, the
> > > colourful plates, or
> > > mouse-grey, namely, passing
> > > water (away from
> > > home), whereas the
> > > bush *blinks* after
> > > Klopstock,

to Titzi to communion, etc., you look like Shirley Temple on the lit. parquet in colour like Shirley Temple in colour how much I dreamt of the avant-garde *painted* so much in the underground, dreamt so much dreamt it all the friends the doves my eyes glued shut in the night but the meadow green and blue and trousers of pure lit. fish what trousers, in Sils Maria too, etc., and painted in Sils Maria painted, what lovely gold of morning, etc., I painted a lot, to my heart's content, dreamt birds feathers the white feathers of a yng. bird already dead and enclosed in its lit. chamber, on the mountains already snow,

> with his hand to his mouth he, showed me that he was hungry, I gave him something to eat (on the blanket, namely, torchlight procession, in blood-red ink!),

was I angry was I angry I bit my tongue, I stamped I stamped my foot, namely, in the a.m., a bouquet of anemones a bouquet of dahlias pale as the evening star so pale, vis-à-vis in the window an open book (or lollipop), I mean, a pale mountain ......

> 18.9.19, I was ill
> and you came to see me,

wolfish, namely, a night-time report, I mean, to wear, a fur hat in summer, those ears of Dürer's hare, I mean, to caress something like (those) *brilliant* ears! that is to caress!, dieu! dieu! under the roof = the Albertina's cap (once), he said what should I read when you've stopped writing then, you're my crutch : heavenly! crutch of cloud : bulging! in the a.m., in the window, once we sat, in winter, on a bench in City Park and all the while slipping out of my moccasins, nevertheless while kissing me (flakes, coiffures) you faded thither, etc., goal of any even the most delicate approach consummate union, namely,

(like jargon),

2.10.19, coming towards
me a man with
blowing white
hair, on a bike, called out
POETRY! which delighted
me, that *during*
the woods I was
rather social like mountain and
snow, like Czech
flowers,

Crust of blood on the lit. mouth I embrace the SCALE

Crust of blood on the lit. mouth I embrace the SCALE, I am
so queer and the GRAMMO says 'mute', at midnight I open
my eyes and wonder why the word SCALE isn't a poetic word
why the word TUMOUR isn't a poetic word, I mean, why
should the words MOON and STAR and SWAN have the
advantage of being poetic words. Snow heap and Robert
Walser there where he once went and died, well yeah, the
zodiac sign LIBRA and that of the HARE, namely, HARE how
it flew across the fields : with a crop, Master Sakai Hōitsu's
Autumn Grasses and Hare with Crop Flying over the Mountains
(all of my relatives had a crop even my sweetest grandmama
too, etc.), the young let themselves be tattooed with roses with
anchors and other symbols of grandeur let their underarms and
breasts be tattooed with scales and hares, you were born a Libra
I am a Hare, hare with crop flying over the mountains ......
curse and annoyance, you say, you say bed-sick and fountains
of heart-coughs, that the lit. bed wetter and wetter, you know,
bent over or kneeling in bed I write everything down, dear me
the autumnal garlands in my head, you are illustrious and His
Serene Highness, I weep my way through the nights (my lan-
guage buried in a bush I have arrived at the goal of my
dreams),

whereas Orion.

the lit. garden the lit. silver garden someone tears off my toes
Mozart's 'A Hand-Kiss' real delicate, I write it down on aca-
demic parquet (already lit. walnut tree! on rusty-red canopy,
behold beloved autumn's arrival!) I whisper 'lit. crown and
hysteria, etc.', *on tippytoes the poem*, you know, *must scamper*, I
mean, chirping, with silver branches : ach the lit. walnut tree
in Schiller Park whereas we from bench to bench, Jacques
Prévert's 'Étranges étrangers' ach the modern in music, rosé
rosé : morning's lit. cheeks, '30s haircuts BUSTY delightful
Grandmother's miraculous blue eyes, nights in the centre city
the chauffeur *cornering* that I imagined : a glorious foreign city,
are we writing poet's poetry?

these daffodils,

                    (my tears in the morning dew the
                    Alpine meadow rejoiced),

according to research from FM : the to-be-read to-be-heard :
now and then in your eyes I read, she was born the same year
as me, looks like a puppet in the park. The doctor said to me
'you will be able to write longer than read', hardly any one read
to me when I was a child : none of them had any time, etc., in
my parent's bookcase 3 volumes of Goethe (behind glass) and
The Good Earth by Pearl S. Buck = the mother's favourite read
...... in the window across the way, in blue I think like one of
my books of poetry, I mean, it could be one of mine but no one
seems to be reading it,

> were I a lit. bird I would wish to be able to
> read, but would console myself with being
> able to fly, perhaps flying is lovelier than
> reading? my first day of school I was asked if
> I could already read? which I answered in the
> affirmative.

A book is a blue carnation I can read the carnation's colour,
you put a wilted carnation into a copy of one of the books I
wrote : although they still smell a bit once wilted, we are
beguiled and seduced, when we read, *when a pale word in a book*,

> we do not want to read any FABLES rather
> narcissism, the rose-vendor, namely, I have
> read a lot of Jacques Derrida's work, had I
> never learnt to read how sad I'd be now,

Elisabeth v. Samsonow has an essay on stuffed animals into which I blissfully succumb, *can you explain the world to me?* a lit. salad leaf : DELIGHTFUL : on the kitchen floor, I wanted, exquisite blackbird, to sit with you at the table as otherwise no one's there, would you like to read to me = sing to me so that I will melt thither, me in a mantle of dust = stabat mater, in such devotion,

18.10.19

dear me : my eye-farewell

3.11.19